Environmental Stress and African Americans

The Other Side of the Moon

GRACE CARROLL

Foreword by Chester M. Pierce
Afterword by Walter Allen

 PRAEGER

Westport, Connecticut
London

Library of Congress Cataloging-in-Publication Data

Carroll, Grace.
  Environmental stress and African Americans : the other side of the
moon / Grace Carroll ; foreword by Chester M. Pierce ; afterword by
Walter Allen.
      p.   cm.
  Includes bibliographical references and index.
  ISBN 0–275–95929–5 (alk. paper)
  1. Afro-Americans—Psychology.   2. Afro-Americans—Social
conditions—1975–   3. Racism—United States—Psychological aspects.
4. United States—Race relations—Psychological aspects.   5. Stress
(Psychology)—United States.   I. Title.
E185.625.C36   1998
305.896′073—DC21   97–5579

British Library Cataloguing in Publication Data is available.

Library of Congress Catalog Card Number: 97–5579
ISBN: 0–275–95929–5

First published in 1998

Praeger Publishers, 88 Post Road West, Westport, CT 06881
An imprint of Greenwood Publishing Group, Inc.

Printed in the United States of America

The paper used in this book complies with the
Permanent Paper Standard issued by the National
Information Standards Organization (Z39.48–1984).

10 9 8 7 6 5 4 3 2 1

To my father, Nathan Joseph Carroll, Sr., who fueled my strong will and showed me how to be a fighter, always keeping my eyes on the prize; to my mother, Masako Murata Carroll, whose unconditional love provided the safety net I needed to take risks and forge ahead with hope; to my brothers, Nathan Joseph Carroll, Jr., and Alan Dalton Carroll, whose support and love for children and family allowed me to be warmly encircled by both; and to my children, Tajai DeNeil and Julana Makiku, whose creative talents, brilliance, and inner beauty fill my life with joy, pride, and laughter, I dedicate this work, done in loving memory of two truly amazing Graces: my paternal grandmother, Grace Anna Carroll, and my cousin, Grace (Jasiri) Ellen Whaley. I love you.

Contents

Foreword

Dr. Grace Carroll has written an educative, absorbing, and persuasive book. She tries to make readers understand the pernicious, destructive effects of racism, which seem omnipresent and ubiquitous in American society. Her method of presentation includes moving autobiographical poetry and prose, as lead-ins for the creative psychosociological research inquiries she has performed.

What may be most special about the book is that it speaks to the important fact that African American investigators are able to conceptualize problem areas in racism, perhaps in a distinctive manner, because of their own life experiences. Dr. Carroll, in addition, takes much care to indicate places of strength in black populations and to give valuable suggestions about how to ameliorate problems and learn more about these issues.

In the general literature on stress much is made about "extreme environments." One might theorize that there are extreme exotic environments and extreme mundane environments. In either end of such a continuum, people would be overwhelmed and in need of massive psychological, biological, and sociological support. Their plight would worsen because of extensive and intensive factors that are aggravated by the unexpected, the uncontrollable, and the unpredictable. Often times, there would be paralyzing indecisiveness and/or dependency preventing a modicum of control over one's space, time, energy, and mobility.

Those habitués of exotic extreme environments are in situations in which, so far, very few people have maneuvered; for example, space travel, or deciding to drop an atom bomb. The habitués of mundane extreme environments can also be under equally disturbing distress. Such habitués—for example, those who have been tortured or terrorized or immobilized in natural or man-made disasters—are in situations that are mundane in the sense that thousands have experienced co-equal circumstances.

In this book the author considers racism as a mundane extreme environment. She describes her own participation as a victim in this circumstance and relates her own personal stories and research studies that are relevant to such victimization. In the United States, she maintains, all blacks suffer from mundane stress, which is unrelenting and never ending.

Many who read these pages will feel indebted to the author. She has an abundance of ideas, particularly ones addressing new avenues of research, parenting skills, and community building. As these ideas are expanded and modified following wider debate, the entire society could benefit from subsequent studies and action programs.

Chester M. Pierce
Harvard University

Preface

Growing up as an African American in the United States, one frequently feels as though one is living in the shadow of whiteness:

> It's ironic that the shadow is black.
> Black—just like me.
> I'm living in that shadow...
> the shadow of whiteness, that is.
> Like a heavy weight—
> the shadow is on me,
> around me,
> everywhere I turn.
> I'm supposed to act like;
> walk like;
> talk like;
> look like;
> feel like,
> those casting the shadow.
> But even when I act like,
> walk like;
> talk like;
> look like...
> why don't I feel like—
> they do?
> Is it because I'm in the shadow
> and the shadow is black?
> Black—just like me.

There are many complexities to living in a non-appreciative environment. If you are black, you really must consider these complexities for survival and success. Too often, it is assumed that living in the shadow is a major burden for all of a darker hue. The burden notwithstanding, many of us rejoice in our differences, our cultural identity and our ethnic origins. Like the other side of the moon, the dark side, we are often overlooked. Yet we also overcome. Given the proper vantage point, the sun does indeed shine on the other side of the moon. We go forward as we become more in tune to our reality and who we are:

> Sitting on the other side of the moon;
> Wondering what it would be like
> to feel the glow and warmth of the light;
> to be seen and admired,
> standing TALL, looking forward;
> viewing my very own reflection,
> relishing in my complexion!
>
> Sitting on the other side of the moon—
> in the shadow, so to speak;
> Wondering how it came to be
> that so few can really see,
> the beauty that I am—
> more precious than any gem.
>
> Sitting on the other side of the moon,
> at times feeling alone and weary,
> tired and rejected...but I do see clearly—
> that I must carry on and bear the weight
> of protecting those before, those present and yet unborn
> from the violence, the untruths and the ungodly scorn
> of those who don't see, don't dare,
> don't care, and don't even understand,
> the beauty in/of me and the beauty I see—
> sitting here, in tune—
> on the other side of the moon.

Too often the story of those of us sitting on the other side of the moon, is not authentically told. Our history and current manifestations of physical as well as psychological violence to African Americans, is replete with examples of how our story is told from the vantage point of those who are not for, nor of us. In this volume I am providing a forum for small groups of African Americans to provide their perspectives on the effects of "living in the shadow of whiteness." I argue that this state of being causes stress and that one must see the light and acknowledge this stress before one can begin taking the necessary steps to successfully move past it.

Acknowledgments

The work involved in completing this book was a joint effort. It includes the voices of many African American fathers, mothers, doctors, lawyers, and students who shared their songs with me and trusted me to record and play them back to you, the reader. I thank them for sharing and particularly for their trust in me.

There are many others I wish to thank. Numerous family members, colleagues, mentors, and friends have encouraged me in my work as a parent and as a professional. They have served as a collective sounding board for my frustrations as well as my triumphs and joys in playing these sometimes competing roles: Wilma and Walter Allen, Debbie Anthony, Bil Banks, Shizuko Barker, Janet and Derrick Bell, Gahiji Bostic, Bernice Brown, Ann Rita and Eldridge Brown, Barbara and John Brown, Robert A. Brown, Wade Boykin, Lorraine Caldwell, Jean Carew, Christia Carroll, Susie and James Carroll, Violetta Carroll, Marie Carter, Alton Chandler, Rebekah Chew, VèVè Clark, Lynn and Tobie Coles, Pat and Bill Dement, Lupe Gallegos-Diaz, Debra and Frank Faté, Bruce Hare, Theresa and Roland Holmes, Cynthia and Willis Holmes, Eugenia and Jay Holmes, JoAnn Intili, Debra and Martin Jacks, Michele and Reginald Jones, Ed Kassam, Keisha and Gary Key, Debbie and Don Lindo, Phyllis and Chandra Lohar-Singh, Ada and John Loper, Charmaine and Dave McIntosh, Dani Monroe, Valata and Leon Monroe, Patricia and Pedro Noguera, Opal Palmer Adisa, Valencia Perkins, Marie Peters, Chet Pierce, Glenn L Robertson, Elmirie Robinson, Columbus Salley, Joy Simmons, Margaret and George Smith, Jai Spriggs, Jere Takahashi, Ula Taylor, Odette and Ewart Thomas, Roy Thomas, Carison Wade, Theresa and Ronniere Whaley, Cahlea and Geleil Whaley, Steve Wilkinson, Michael Woodard, and Yolanda Zesati.

Finally, one of the blessings of working in a university setting is the fact that you get to meet, teach, and learn from so many gifted students. I wish to give a general thanks to all of the U.C. Berkeley students who have put so much time into making a positive difference in the African American experience on that campus. During my decade at U.C. Berkeley, many students helped me in getting this book together by completing tasks ranging from checking bibliographic references to data collection. In particular, I would like to say a special thanks to those who have spent their time on this project: Mia B., Ingrid Banks, Kena Bell, Kelley Bradshaw, Ainka Fulani, Nicole Harper, Chinyere Inyama, Deirdre Johnson, Hilda Barnes Kennedy, Felicia Law, Maisha Simmons, Karolyn Tyson, Mat Wambua, Sheila Williams, and Jesse Williamson. The Creator has blessed me to have each of you in my life.

1

Introduction: African Americans and Mundane Extreme Environmental Stress

17 January. The last Martin Luther King holiday the nation would ever observe dawned on an extraordinary sight. In the night, the Space Traders had drawn their strange ships right up to the beaches and discharged their cargoes of gold, minerals, and machinery, leaving vast empty holds. Crowded on the beaches were the inductees, some twenty million silent black men, women, and children, including babes in arms. As the sun rose, the Space Traders directed them, first, to strip off all but a single undergarment; then, to line up; and finally, to enter those holds which yawned in the morning light like Milton's "darkness visible." The inductees looked fearfully behind them. But, on the dunes above the beaches, guns at the ready, stood U.S. guards. There was no escape, no alternative. Heads bowed, arms now linked by slender chains, black people left the New World as their forebears had arrived.

—Derrick Bell
Faces at the
Bottom of the Well

INTRODUCTION

This book shares perspectives in an effort to create understanding. It explains how African Americans negotiate their day-to-day lives under the "shadow of whiteness." It offers the reader the oppportunity to listen to the many black voices of those who *really believe* that America would gladly get rid of us if given the space trader opportunity: trading African Americans for materials and technology. I have taken a nontraditional approach to this effort by merging creative, autobiographical, and empirical writings. Thus, in each of the following chapters, the reader will find my own personal vignettes plus the voices of others who, too, share the experience of being black in an often hostile environment. Their voices are shared in a series of qualitative, empirical studies. This first chapter, however, presents a very brief historical backdrop and the theoretical foundation upon which the vignettes and studies are precariously erected.

BACKGROUND

As a college student in the sixties, I, like many of my contemporaries, was filled with the hope that one day we would realize Martin Luther King's dream of every person being judged by the content of his or her character instead of the color of his or her skin. However, the events and experiences of the past three decades have led many African Americans to reassess our position and strategies for survival and success in these United States. From the Rodney King incident where an unarmed motorist was captured on videotape being severely beaten by police officers, who were acquitted of their crimes, to the Texaco executive boardroom where qualified African Americans were labeled "black jelly beans" and faced firsthand the pain of crashing against the "glass ceiling," the pressures of being African American in an environment where skin color is still the most dominant criterion of evaluation has taken, and continues to take, a serious toll. This is particularly so for African Americans because blackness is so highly devalued and degraded as a racial category in this country. It is seen as the opposite of the value placed on whiteness according to a personal mentor and friend, Derrick Bell. He, too, once shared the vision of Martin Luther King, Jr. particularly as he worked with diligence in the arena of civil rights jurisprudence to help get the necessary laws in place to ensure "equal treatment" for all people. However, in one of his books, *Faces at the Bottom of the Well*, he shares a story entitled "Space Traders," from which this chapter's opening excerpt was taken. In this story, law-abiding white America decides to exchange its African Americans for financial and technological payment from space traders. In speaking with students, colleagues, and friends, both black and white, who have read "Space Traders" a curious dilemma begins to unfold as this story is discussed. Many state directly that yes, white America would have no problems trading in its African Americans. Others, however, begin speaking of the impracticality of the story—for example, they ask, how could one get all African Americans in one place to board the ships? or how unlikely is it that African Americans wouldn't put up a stronger fight? or even how could you tell who is "really" African American with all of the miscegenation over the years? It is almost as though the knowledge that such a choice could possibly be made makes for a level of uncomfortability, forcing one to seek out alternative levels of discussion. This then enables one to avoid the obvious point of the allegory: that if given the opportunity, many whites would gladly make this trade; that African Americans are seen as dispensable.

Bell's contemporary writings reiterate W.E.B. Du Bois' (1903) most quoted statement, that the most pressing problem facing America in the twentieth century is that of the color line. This statement is used so frequently because as we approach the twenty-first century, the *problem* of how we perceive, define, and negotiate "race" [1] is *still* a major one. For social science researchers, instead of becoming more manageable, the color line problem seems to have become even more complex. Why is it that in 1997, over a century after slavery was abolished, and almost a century after Du Bois wrote, people of African descent still feel like outcasts in America?

This feeling of being unwanted in America, the stigma of being African in a society dominated by anti-African thought and Eurocentric ideas of beauty, dominance, and entitlement, creates a unique stress for African Americans. This stress is present in all identifiable African Americans and/or all who identify with being of African descent. It is a common thread weaving together all African Americans of every socioeconomic and professional level, across all political persuasions and ideological orientations. As evidence of the pervasiveness of this stress factor, I conduct classes and workshops and put on a variety of presentations to African American groups. I often start out with the following three questions:

1.   Have you ever been the only African American person in a class or meeting and a so-called black issue comes up and suddenly you feel all eyes are on you—that you are supposed to have the "appropriate response"?—that you can speak for *all* African Americans?

2.   Have you ever watched the news and a particularly violent crime is described and your first reaction is: "God, I hope the perpetrator is not black"?

3.   Have you even been in a store, bar, or restaurant and felt you were next in line for service only to see that a white patron got served instead?

Inevitably, African Americans answer yes to each of these three questions. Respondents have each in their own way experienced the emotional stressful feelings that come with being African American in the context of a society that, too frequently, denies our positive existence and takes every opportunity to expose and create anything negative. Yes, the murders of Nicole Simpson and Ronald Goldman were brutal and wrong, but is it necessary to take surveys of O.J.'s guilt or innocence and then make black/white comparisons? Did we take such racial poles in the Dahmer killings? Our society is still so obsessed by "race" that we tend to racialize everything, particularly black/white issues. African Americans are, however, constantly accused of "playing the race card"; yet, the fact is the race card is played each and every day in a variety of forms by

---

[1] In his forthcoming book, *The 100 Must Read for African Americans: From the African Past to Today*, Dr. Columbus Salley concurs with past scholars in questioning the validity and the "science" of "race" and "race classifications" in explaining human diversity. The book on this in his "must read" list is Ashley Montagu's *Man's Most Dangerous Myth: The Fallacy of Race*. Both authors argue that "race" was constructed by Europeans to justify inhuman behavior to "nonwhites." Thus, the use of the word "race" is problematic and misleading.

nonblacks. In the O.J. Simpson trial, the race card was played by NBC, ABC, CBS, and CNN far in advance of its being played by O.J.

One of my mentors, Dr. Chester Pierce, describes this atmosphere as a mundane extreme environment: an environment in which racism and subtle oppression are ubiquitous, constant, continuing, and mundane and one in which African Americans must daily suffer the annoying "micro-aggressions" such environments breed (Pierce 1970, 1974). Examples of micro-aggressions include being ignored for service; assumed to be guilty of anything negative; treated as inferior; stared at because of color; ridiculed because of hair texture; singled out because of our differences, ad infinitum. We have labeled the stress of living in such an environment accordingly, mundane extreme environmental stress (M.E.E.S.): mundane, because this stress is so common and is so much a part of our day-to-day experience that we almost take it for granted; extreme, because it has an extreme impact on our psyche and worldview, how we see ourselves, behave, interact, and so forth; environmental, because it is environmentally induced and fostered; stress, because the ultimate impact on African Americans is indeed stressful, detracting, and energy consuming.

One just needs to review the history of Africans in America to document the atrocities and inhumane treatment of slaves and the subsequent institutional, scientific, and personal racism leading to continued inequities between African Americans and other Americans, to understand the foundation of mundane extreme environmental stress. To document the history that created and incubated the circumstances for M.E.E.S. is not the purpose of this volume. Many historians, anthropologists, sociologists, and psychologists have written profound and descriptive accounts of this "peculiar institution" and its results (America 1990; Drake 1945; Genovese 1979; Stamp 1956; Woodson 1933). Understanding the environment in which African Americans live, work, and play, however, is critical in understanding the M.E.E.S. with which every African American must contend, and thus, a very brief contextual frame is presented in the following section.

RACISM: THE FOUNDATION FOR M.E.E.S.

The history of the treatment, perceptions, and images projected of African Americans has led to the incubation and full development of the M.E.E.S. factor in each and every aspect of life for black Americans. In an article, "The Politics of Family in America," which appeared in a special issue of *Nation* (1989:116-22), Jewell Handy Gresham provided a succinct link between an early account of how African Americans were viewed by the "powers that be" and images that are perpetrated today. I was struck by the consistency of the message that African Americans are pathological and how data were (and still are) manipulated, and in some cases fabricated, to add the necessary fuel to burn the fire of racism. Dr. Gresham pointed out the following:

• In 1844 Secretary of State John Calhoun, in a letter, stated that where blacks and whites existed in the same society, slavery was the natural result. Wherever the state changed that providential relationship, the blacks invariably degenerated "into vice and pauperism accompanied by bodily and mental afflictions incident thereto—deafness, blindness, insanity and idiocy." In slave states, in contrast, the blacks improved greatly, "in number, comfort, intelligence and morals." He cited 1840 census data to prove his point—data showing a shocking rate of black insanity in New England (i.e., 1:14 in Maine, etc.) versus only 1:1309 in Virginia. Dr. Edward Jarvis of the Massachusetts General Hospital, a leading specialist in the incidence of insanity, in conjunction with the American Statistical Association (A.S.A.) proved this to be a lie. Calhoun's letter got to Congress; the A.S.A. report did not.

- In the book, *The Plantation Negro as Freeman* by historian Philip A. Bruce (1889), a former Virginia slave owner, the major thesis is that with the loss of white supervision, severe and menacing deterioration of the black social and moral condition would occur—for black children were born into a state of moral degeneracy. He particularly attacked the black women—they were raped and failed to complain so this was proof of the sexual laxness of plantation women. His work was the important connecting link between the "popular views" of African American degeneracy in the 1880s and the supportive, pseudoscientific data of social Darwinism, which justified the decades of violent racism that followed.

- The 1964 Patrick Moynihan report served the same purpose as Calhoun's—to shift the focus on real systemwide problems due to racism to the pathology of the black family. His report centered on the matriarchal pathology in black families and his solution was "benign neglect."

- Bill Moyers picked up the ball on January 25, 1986, with the prime time TV special, "The Vanishing Black Family—Crisis in Black America." He received the Alfred I. DuPont-Columbia University Gold Baton for the program which was judged to have made the greatest contribution to the public's understanding of an important issue. It focused on teens parents and the pathology of the black family and concluded with a victim-blame framework: if these families and teens just knew better they could get themselves together.

- President Ronald Reagan stated: "The solution to the crime problem will not be found in the social worker's files, the psychiatrist's notes or the bureaucrat's budget—only our deep moral values and strong institutions can hold back that jungle and restrain the darker impulses of human nature."

- President Geroge Bush in 1988, addressed the Republican Governors Association in Alabama (under the Confederate flag, which hangs in the state capitol), and he committed himself to building more prisons.

Calhoun and Bruce used the terms "moral degenerate," "sexual laxness," "insanity," and "menacing deterioration." These terms do not seem much different than Moynihan, and Reagan's use of terms "pathological," "jungle," "moral values," and "darker impulses." Both sets of leaders appear to agree on three fronts. First, they believe that African Americans are naturally deficient and pathological.   Second, they agree African Americans need to be enslaved, whether on a plantation or in ghetto areas and prisons. Finally, they agree that one can use and abuse data through misinterpretation, partial reporting, and/or inventing it and passing it off as accurate. One then can use such data to build a case to further institutional racism. Clearly, this is a reason for stress if you are the target of these negative data sets.

There is not a quantum leap between the thoughts and ensuing policies of the leaders of the 1800s and those of today.   However, over two centuries have elapsed since these enlightened leaders made their justifications for black inferiority.   These pseudoscientific pronouncements were piled on top of two previous centuries of slavery. Thus, African Americans have suffered four centuries of victimization by such false assumptions, misinterpretations, allegations, and resulting policy; four centuries of unequal treatment, physical and psychological brutality; four centuries for a massive rejection of what is African and holding in high esteem what is European; four centuries for African Americans to become accustomed to being in the shadow of white America.   There are those who would argue that these four centuries have more than provided the time and foundation for an effective self-fulfilling prophecy to occur within the African American community: one where African Americans have come to accept that "white like is right" and blackness represents badness (Russell, Wilson, and Hall 1992). Needless to say, there is an overabundance of indicators that stress and being African American are inextricably tied together.   To say that being black in America doesn't add a high stress factor is to be blind to the history and contemporary manifestations of that history.   To ignore this stress factor (M.E.E.S.) is to not face the facts and thus isolate oneself from strategies to successfully manage and negotiate the inevitable.

THE "BLACK = BAD" EQUATION

Based on this history of racism and "colorism," children socialized in America with any identifiable African blood have three strikes against them, according to psychologist Dr. Naim Akbar (1984).   These three strikes are represented by the three factors that Akbar suggests separate African Americans from other racial groups in America:

1.   The involuntary immigration and the resulting form of slavery to which blacks were subjugated
2.   The physical features and coloring of blacks that, like castes, make membership by birth
3.   The fact that African/African American culture is not respected in this country and thus is used as a source of shame rather then a source of empowerment

The interplay of these factors, resting on their foundation of racism, creates in America the ominous and deadly association of blackness/African with negativity.   This negative association has been well documented in a wide variety of sources—from folklore to research. The whole tradition of the good guys in white, the bad guys in black, including the Clarks' study and recent replications of their study where white dolls were preferred over black ones, sadly points to the perpetuation and acceptance of the "Black = Bad" equation (Clark and Clark 1958). The historical mass acceptance of this equation creates particular and peculiar social and psychological problems for African Americans and fosters M.E.E.S. Pierce (1969) wrote, the most oppressing aspect of M.E.E.S. and the acceptance of the "Black = Bad" equation is,

[I don't] believe that many blacks can live a total hour of their conscious life without recognizing the fact of their blackness and being reminded of it in all sorts of ways— every black has to be hung up in these issues.

One might argue that "hung up" may be a bit strong. Yet, most African Americans will agree that we are reminded of race each and every day: on TV, in the newspaper, on the street, at the workplace, in school. We do not all respond to these reminders in the same way, but we do in fact respond in some way.

SYMBOLIC INTERACTION: WHY WE ACT AND THINK THE WAY WE DO

An understanding of the reasons why so many of us have bought into the "Black = Bad" equation and why so many African Americans experience M.E.E.S. needs developing. Clearly history is an important factor. However, there are theoretical bases for why people think the way they do and subsequently behave the way they do. One such theoretical framework is symbolic interaction (Cooley 1902; Mead 1934), which is important in our understanding of how "race" is factored into our daily lives. Because looking black is the first visual cue that others have when dealing with black people, it becomes a very potent criterion regarding thought and action. Symbolic interactionism underscores the importance of the way one looks (phenotype) and assumes that your perception of how others view you has a great impact on how you view yourself. What follows is a brief overview of key theoretical constructs of symbolic interaction. This provides a theoretical construct for the importance of phenotype (looking African) in self-conception. It also provides for the theoretical underpinnings of mundane extreme environmental stress.

The symbolic interactionist tradition stresses the significance of societal influence upon an individual. Consequently, human behavior is a result of *interaction* with one's environment, beyond direct reaction to it. Sociologist George H. Mead (1934), often considered the father of the symbolic interactionist tradition, capsulated this distinction by contrasting human to nonhuman behavior. He concludes that nonhuman gestures do not carry the connotation of conscious meaning or intent, but serve merely as cues for the appropriate responses of others. On the other hand, humans engage in *meaningful* gestures (speech and other symbols). In so doing, humans interject interpretations which may lead to varying responses to others dependent on these interpretations (Mead 1934). In other words, in human interaction one takes the role of any given actor in order to *interpret* the gestures of the actor. These interpretations lead to the response to that actor as depicted below :

person X ⟶ person Y ⟶ person Y
emits gesture (Sl)   interprets the gesture Sl (YSl)   replies to interpretation YSl

According to this view of behavior, humans respond to the interpretation of the gestures of others, to what we believe the gesture means. For example, if a white salesperson in a clothing store served a white customer before she served you, a black woman, you might interpret her behavior as racist because you were there first and because of your past history with whites who have ignored you for service. If you do make this interpretation, you may get angry and your facial expressions may show this anger. You have a valid reason to interpret her behavior as racist, given the history and relationship between whites and blacks and the regularity of racist behavior directed toward you. However, the salesperson may not have known you were first in line for service. She may interpret your anger as your being inconsiderate or "typical, hostile, black behavior."

Manis and Meltzer (1967), in their discussion of Mead's work on symbolic interaction emphasized that the

...relation of human beings to one another arises from the developed ability of the human beings to respond to his own gestures. This ability enables different human beings to respond in the same way, to the same gestures, thereby sharing one another's experience; behavior is viewed as "social" not simply when it is a response to others, but rather when it has incorporated it in the behavior of others.

In other words humans can create a "social reality." If enough people are convinced through interaction with one another that this social reality is "real," then for all practical purposes, it becomes reality. Thus, if there exists a stereotype of black inferiority and one believes this stereotype, one acts accordingly.

The preceding arguments assume the presence of a "self." Mead loosely described the development of this self, through his "I", "me" formulations. The "me" is symbolic of the incorporated other within the individual, that acts to direct the "I" impulses. Thus, everyone develops a sense of whom he or she is by the interaction of one's natural impulses or instincts ("I"), with how he or she interprets and incorporates his or her interaction with the environment ("me"). The interpretations an individual makes can depend on a specific interaction with a specific person in the environment or with the "generalized other." The generalized other is one's perception of how persons *in general* feel about any given act, object, person(s), thought, or response. The assumption is that this perception of the generalized other's views is also very important in developing a "self." In the context of the sociopolitical landscape of America, whites view themselves as superior to blacks because they have incorporated the views of the society (generalized other) regarding blacks into their own sense of self. Conversely, blacks who are in the same general social context of black-devaluated status may also incorporate this devaluation into their own sense of self. A person's sense of self may be viewed as a compository of his or her perceptions of how others (both specific and generalized) view him or her.

The stark reality of how African Americans are viewed collectively in a negative manner is reflected in the research literature on identity formation. The distinction between one's personal identity and one's reference group identity is often made for African Americans (Jackson, McCollough, and Gurin 1988). The case is made that for some African Americans to see themselves as positive, they have to make a split between themselves and the larger African American community. The assumption is that the African American community is viewed negatively and thus in order to have high self-esteem, you have to separate your personal identity (I am a good person) from the often negative collective black identity (black people, in general, are not good). Clearly, in the best of all worlds, such a separation should not have to occur in order to have a positive "self." This state of affairs can surely add to the M.E.E.S. factor of the individual who perceives that he or she must make such a separation.

Prior to Mead, another social scientist, Cooley (1902), was noted for his concept, the "looking glass self." He asserted that the "sense of self" is a precondition for people to have control of their environment, and that this control is a desired state by the actors involved. Like Mead, Cooley believed the sense of self is an outgrowth of interaction within a given social context. Cooley based his theory on the following assumptions:

1. People's behavior elicits judgments from others.
2. People imagine the judgments of others in reaction to their behavior and thoughts.
3. The imagined judgments of others are incorporated into and comprise the various aspects of a person's sense of self.
4. People's behavior reflects their sense of self.
5. Different others are perceived as judging behaviors in different ways.
6. The imagined judgments of the others are more likely to be incorporated into the person's sense of self if the imagined judgments are from individuals who are particularly important to the person.
7. People will more likely behave in such a way to receive the imagined positive judgment of important others rather than unimportant others.

Cooley incorporated the idea of "significant" others. Some people are either more rewarding, influential, and/or important in the development of the "sense of self" than others. For example, if you are in a position to give rewards or punishment to a person, you are a significant other to that person. In America, societal rewards, such as good jobs and the opportunity to get a good education and recognition, are most often in the hands of whites. Thus, their evaluations become significant to those dependent on such rewards.

Based on this symbolic interactionist tradition, the way one looks, or the ethnic/cultural group with which one identifies, becomes a critical variable in how African Americans are perceived and responded to by both specific and generalized others. This consequently influences how blacks view themselves and how they act toward others. In a society where the "Black = Bad" equation is still very much believed, one could hypothesize that a child who has more white physical attributes (i.e. skin color, hair texture, facial features, etc.) may accrue certain favorable responses that elude the child with more African American physical attributes; or the person who "acts" more white will be valued more than one who relates more closely to African cultural norms. There are, however, various mediating variables, such as type of home environment, educational setting, parents' perspectives, and so on, that can make a difference in self-perception. Such mediating variables can buffer or reshape the impact of one's personal response to the "Black = Bad" equation.

In addition to an individual's personal response via symbolic interaction, there are many structural issues that must be considered when analyzing mundane extreme environmental stress. Barriers to equal educational opportunities, job discrimination, housing options and unequal access to quality services in a vast array of areas, all contribute to M.E.E.S. They set in motion, support and affirm the "Black = Bad" equation. For example, in one of the following chapters, black men share how very important it is to have a job in order to successfully fulfill the father role in America. Structural variables such as lack of quality education coupled with discrimination in employment, result in disproportionate numbers of African American men who are unemployed, underemployed, or who just do not believe they can get a job and thus have given up (Hacker 1992). Many of them look at themselves as reflections in the societal mirror that say unemployed black men are mere negative statistics. It is very stressful to carry such a burden and can lead to many maladaptive and even self-destructive behaviors. Thus, the societal depiction and treatment of African Americans and our families, institutionalized in the social and political system, often has major impacts on how we view ourselves and interact with each other.

FUELING M.E.E.S.:   THEORY AND RESEARCH ON BLACK FAMILIES

One example of how African Americans have been depicted in a very negative light is evident in the research and theories about our families. Noted sociologist, Walter Allen (1978) described three models used to conceptualize and conduct family research: cultural deviant, cultural equivalent, and cultural variant. It is my contention that each of these models assumes a symbolic interactionist foundation. In the cultural deviant model, Eurocentric models of behaviors, attitudes, and family structure are used as the ideal standard by which all other groups are compared. When these others "fall short" of the standard, "deviance," "pathological," and other such negatively charged labels are descriptors called upon to account for the differences. Such a model was the basis for the Calhoun, Reagan, and Moyers's descriptions of African Americans. The cultural equivalent model, like the deviance model, assumes the correctness of the

Eurocentric model; however, the differences are accounted for by such mitigating factors as lack of opportunity, or economic disparities. Certain affirmative action programs often use this model: if we just give black people more of a chance they will be just like white people. The cultural variant model, on the other hand, does not assume one universal model of cultural correctness or appropriateness. It suggests that different cultures have different cultural mandates, and if nurtured and allowed to develop on their own, different cultures would develop various functional patterns of behaviors, attitudes and structures. It takes the unorthodox approach of suggesting that different cultures are indeed different and that difference is okay, not deviant, not on the bottom rung of a ladder leading to Eurocentric heights, but on a different, equally valid path.

Unfortunately, studies focusing on black families and black people in general have been fragmented and typically have been pejorative. The cultural deviant models have predominated. Until recently most have viewed black families as deviant and problem prone. Research has not been very concerned with describing and analyzing actual everyday behaviors, attitudes, and coping mechanisms of African Americans within an ecological and functional perspective (Billingsley 1968, 1992; Boykin 1979; Mathis 1978; Peters 1978). Nor has this research looked at the activities of African Americans from our vantage points and perspectives. I emphasize the plural here because African American families are not monolithic and our internal diversity must also be considered in this research. There is very little in the research literature that takes the M.E.E.S. factor into account when describing or analyzing the circumstances of African Americans.

The exclusion of the special needs, issues, and stresses of black families in the conceptualization of stress-related research is one example of the subtle and elusive nature of institutional racism within American culture. It can been seen as a metaphor for our exclusion from the day-to-day life in America (Ellison 1952). As an outgrowth of the prevailing negative approach implicit in the omission of blacks from many normative studies, observations and considerations of behavior in black families have rarely been examined within the concepts of family stress theory. In addition to studies of stress caused by extreme traumatic events (Wolf and Mosnaim 1990), there have been studies of chronic role stress (Pearlin 1983) and daily hassle stress (Kanner et al 1987). However, these fail to address race as the critical factor interweaving all of these threads, the fact that there is a daily hassle in the constant role of just being black. There has been no formal recognition of the mundane extreme environmental stress black families experience. There has been little, if any, recognition of the cumulative effects of the micro-aggressions to which blacks are daily subjugated via media and day to day interactions on the job and in the general public. This general public has been racialized by a unique American history and its consequent structural circumstances; and the burdens of this history weigh heavily on African Americans.

An early potential for recognizing and understanding M.E.E.S. was probably deflected by the politically motivated issues of the 1960s that focused public attention on "poverty amidst affluence." As a result, much of the post-sixties research on black families developed out of the "War on Poverty" frame of reference. Concepts such as "cycles of poverty," "disorganization," and "pathological," highlighted in the Department of Labor's Moynihan report, are typical of research and writings regarding black families (Mathis 1978; Peters 1978). Black families that differed from mainstream America were considered to be deviant, illegitimate, and/or deteriorating and thus pathological. This label of "deviance" contributed to the misfocusing of much of the research of the sixties and early seventies involving black families (Mathis 1978).

As a reaction to this critical and damaging research, a number of writers and social scientists began to point to the "strengths" of black families, strengths that enabled us to survive despite poverty, racism, and discrimination (Aschenbrenner 1975; Hill 1972; Nobles 1976; Peters 1976, 1978; Stack 1974; Staples 1976). This early literature provided the basis for analysis of coping behaviors in black families. Coping behaviors can be viewed as a combination of adaptation and response to the continuing stress of perpetual and pervasive racism. By examining personal environment, interpersonal relationships, family interactions, and family-community relationships, the various strategies that allow racism to be absorbed, deflected, combated, and/or overcome by particular black families and individuals can be studied. By exploring various personal or family attempts to cope with M.E.E.S. (the "normal," stressful, everyday situations of racism, discrimination, or personal humiliation, and the extreme stress of sudden eruptions or racial crises), the regenerative power of black and other oppressed families can be better understood.

In the eighties and nineties, the cultural deviant models of research and analysis merged with popular media's new thrust of "real world" docudrama. These docudramas often perpetuated all of the negative stereotypes held by the majority viewing audience. No longer was the academic deviant perspective of African American families limited to so-called scholarly journals. Now in living color, Bill Moyers was projecting this model to millions on prime time TV in a two-hour special appropriately titled, "The Vanishing Black Family." Not only were we getting bombarded with African American men in handcuffs and mug shots on the 6:00 news, but also in real life television series such as "America's Most Wanted," "911," and "Cops." As the economy got worse and competition for goods and services got fierce, the cultural deviant model was far outpacing the cultural equivalent model. White Americans no longer felt they had the luxury of giving a helping hand to those less fortunate if they happen to be black. They believed that the two decades of affirmative action should have erased the nearly four centuries of inequalities, and put African Americans on equal footing. Indeed, in California the populace acted on this assumption of equality and voted to end all programs that give preferences based on race or gender.[2] Cries of re-

---

[2] This was done in the form of a state proposition (Proposition 209). Its promoters called it the "Civil Rights Initiative" and its opponents dubbed it the "Civil Wrongs Initiative" because it called for an end to all programs that use race or gender for preference. The voters passed it.

verse discrimination became in vogue and were loud enough for court support. Needless to say, the mundane extreme environmental stress factor reached new heights.

The conceptual framework for much stress and coping research today is based on a typology of family crisis that describes a family's reaction to or handling of a sudden or new stressful event that occurs either (1) within the family and caused by a family member, or (2) outside the family and is caused by a catastrophe, such as tornado damage, economic depression, war, or father's absence. The model focuses on newness, suddenness, and/or severity of crises, family vulnerability, and the family's regenerative power. A family's reaction is dependent upon the type of crisis, its duration, and which members created the crisis (Hill 1963). This perspective, however, is conceptually limiting for it does not accommodate situations of continued, ongoing oppression such as mundane extreme environmental stress, within which periodic but unpredictable stressful events and demands for sudden change can be expected to occur. Families negotiating M.E.E.S. differ from families whose homes, for example, are located in an area subject to periodic flooding, or from families who operate a farm in a drought-prone area of the country, or from families in which income is dependent upon a job in an occupational field subject to seasonal layoffs. In these situations the stressful event is anticipated and reactions and resources can be programmed for mobilization when necessary. It is only the timing of the stressful event that is uncertain. At other times, life goes on as usual. Unless the family belongs to a cultural/ethnic group which is devalued in the society such as African Americans, the undergirding effect and influence of M.E.E.S. is absent. For example, when a black family's home is destroyed, as were the homes of my friends, the Monroes and the Browns, in the 1990 Oakland firestorm, their stress also included the special problems a black family may face in locating another desirable place to live or getting appropriate services by agencies set up to help the fire victims. Will the housing counselor be fair? Will the insurance adjuster try to give them less than other firestorm victims? Will the family be referred to an undesirable low-income neighborhood for housing? Will the black family encounter hostility moving into an integrated or "white" neighborhood? An analysis of a stress situation for black families must include recognition of the subtle influence race may have on their recovery potential and how M.E.E.S. plays into the scenario. If the additional stress and coping strategies and resources reflective of M.E.E.S. are incorporated in the study of African Americans, such studies become more comprehensive and, of course, more applicable to the lives of African Americans.

The unique situation of African American families suggests the need for family stress theories and studies to be conceptualized within a framework that would include recognition of two additional stress factors for minority families. There is (1) the extreme but mundane stress of omnipresent racism (M.E.E.S.) described above, and there is (2) the chronic and often unpredictable racially caused stressful events encountered throughout the life cycle. These sources of stress, whether mundane or chronic and crisis producing are in addition to the kinds of family stress that other families may occasionally encounter.

The types and resources of black families and individuals best equipped to meet the continuing and changing onslaughts of racism need to be known. What are the characteristics of family organization, interpersonal networks and coping strategies that can aid in positively channeling and deflecting the impact of racism? What type of actions contribute to the reduction of negative effects of racism on black families, especially their children? How do African Americans foster and achieve upward mobility, maintain healthy personalities, and learn how to handle racial identity-related stresses (M.E.E.S)? Each of these questions is rich with research possibilities. Further, it would be instructive to explore the course of adjustment to racial stress as new situations emerge throughout the life cycle, to describe the variety of strategies families use, and to document how families socialize and teach children to survive under continued overt and covert racial oppression. A few families and individuals will share their answers to these questions in the following chapters.

LIVING WITH M.E.E.S.

The African American family structure and black extended friendship networks may be arenas for tensions and frustrations, but they are also the domains for the resolution of these tensions and frustrations (McAdoo 1980). The use of the family as a critical coping strategy has been described by a number of researchers (McAdoo 1988). According to sociologist (1976), African American families provide a sanctuary that buttresses their members from the pervasiveness of oppression and racism. Whether in the realm of strategies for survival, mutually reciprocal kin/friendship support, or maintenance of emotional well-being, Staples suggested that factors embedded in black values, as reflected in the family system, must be accounted for in any discussion of the stresses of life for African Americans. This perspective is also seen in the research of psychologist Wade Nobles (1976: 181), who examined the way in which "the black family structure and functions serve to support its members in their dealings with an overtly hostile and racist wider society." A related branch of studies adopts an ecological perspective wherein black families are viewed as viable, functional, and interacting within an African American community encapsulated within American mainstream society (Aschenbrenner 1975; Coner-Edwards and Spurlock 1988; Davidson 1978; Gay 1972; Hill 1972; Martin and Martin 1978; McAdoo 1978; Peters 1976; Stack 1974). Researchers have described African American family life and identified coping strategies that have allowed their survival in the given environment of M.E.E.S. This approach assumes that most African American families have developed patterns of behaviors, attitudes and practices that are appropriate to the values and constraints within their own lives. Too often, sensitive, insightful, informed research is missing from mainstream literature and policy development. Negative maladaptive behavior, instead of positive adaptive behavior, is often the focus of the literature and its portrayal of African Americans.

I have argued for inclusion of mundane extreme environmental stress when describing or analyzing data or situations involving African Americans. It is unfortunate that in every arena, African Americans must factor in a race variable. Thus, when a black person marries a white person, or when a black woman straightens her hair, or when a black man wins an election, or when a black child is involved in a crime, or when a black student gets good grades, or when a black child is born to a teenager, or when a black man kills a white, ad nauseum, it is never merely a personal triumph or defeat. It is a politically charged event. Politicians, media, and the public in general play the infamous race card. Given this history of race relations and racism, African Americans are constantly bearing the burden of reacting to (acceptance or rejection) white standards, white comparisons, and white evaluations. The title of Guthrie's book, *Even the Rat Was White* (1976), is indicative of the pervasiveness of "whiteness" in the lives of black people. This living within the shadow of whiteness is stressful and time consuming.

The purpose of this volume is to explore the M.E.E.S. factor in a variety of settings and its impact on the thoughts and actions of African Americans. Each chapter examines a different environment in which a selected group of African Americans live, work, and play. Each chapter provides a voice to African Americans whose stories have not often been told from their vantage point, for example, black fathers who *do* take responsibility for their children. These respondents share their daily battles with M.E.E.S.; their concerns and fears; their triumphs and joys. They also describe their various coping mechanisms. In addition, I use my own personal developmental experiences, from growing up in a family that did not fit the stereotype, to being subjected to the special racial stresses which accompany being a professional black woman, as music for the singing of the lyrics composed by many of my clients, students, peers, and friends. As African Americans, our experiences are at times harmonious and at other times in discord with one another. Yet, these rhythms are intricately interwoven. We have a powerful song to sing.

2

Of M.E.E.S. and Men: Case Studies of African American Single Fathers

INTRODUCTION

My experiences with African American men began with my father and two brothers. These experiences were nothing like the images of African American men projected in the media: the pimps, junkies, and winos; the vivid scenes of men being arrested on the 6:00 news and the barrage of negative statistics concerning our men constantly being paraded on TV. Quite the contrary, the men in my family are hard-working African American men, struggling to make a decent living and good homes for their families and friends. My father fought each day so that the racism in the army would not get the best of him. I know it was difficult, as I witnessed him take more than his fair share of micro-aggressions in this military environment. I lived through his bouts with alcohol, which was his way of temporarily escaping the pressures. I saw his health deteriorate and finally felt that he wanted help, but just did not know how to ask. He is a very proud black man.

One afternoon, when he had a bit too much to drink, I, with my mother's help, took him to an alcohol treatment center. We forced him to stay and since drinking made him sleepy, he obliged by going to sleep in one of the rooms in the treatment center. Around two a.m., I got a phone call from my dad. He could not believe we had left him at the center. He demanded that I come and pick him up. I told him that I would not pick him up and that he needed to understand and acknowledge that he was a functional alcoholic and needed help. He was angry and said he would get one of his friends to pick him up. I hung up the phone, woke my mother, and asked for the phone numbers of my dad's few friends. I called them all in that early morning hour, and told them to please not respond if my dad called them for a ride. The next morning my dad called. I asked him about his night at the center and whether or not he had followed through by calling a friend to pick him up. He said no. I then informed him that I had called all of his friends that night. He was silent. I believe he was so embarrassed that he stayed in the treatment center the full three weeks of the residential program. That was in 1981. He has not had a drink of alcohol since. He went on to learn how to enjoy his retirement from the army without alcohol and graduated from the local junior college with a better grade point average than I got in college. His diet is totally changed and he now, in retirement, walks five miles a day with my mother. My dad had the guts to go to battle with the mundane stress of being a responsible black man every day. My dad had the strength and determination to quit drinking after thirty years. My dad never shirked his responsibilities to his children. My dad always had at least one job; more often, two. He modeled this behavior to his sons, who each have graduated from college and are responsible for the welfare of their children. It is critical for us not to overlook men like those in my family, who in spite of all the negativity, still walk tall and embrace the role of father the best way they can.

Mundane extreme environmental stress (M.E.E.S.) plays a critical role in the lives of such African American men who must constantly deal with the negative images and stereotypes projected, plus the fear and animosity directed toward them from the society at large. Moreover, M.E.E.S. is compounded for African American single fathers who are the focus of this chapter. They are subjected to a triple stress: being single in a society where having a partner is more socially accepted and financially secure; being single fathers in a society that is more accustomed to dealing with the issues facing single mothers; and being African American men in a society that has a history of excessive oppression toward black men (Marable 1982, 1991).

The purpose of this chapter is to explore the special circumstances of responsible African American single fathers, to tell a story too often forgotten, of the black men who do take their paternal responsibilities seriously. A small case study in which ten African American fathers who each share or provide solely the primary care-giving responsibility of raising their children is the vehicle by which this story will be shared. However, before presenting this story, it is important and necessary to briefly review the context in which the lives of African American men unfold, the day-to-day circumstances and the M.E.E.S. factor, which they must confront living in America.

CONTEXT

During the past decade there has been a significant increase in the number of single parent households headed by men. This population grew from 600,000 in 1980 to nearly one million by 1990 (Grief and Demaris 1990; 259-67. Despite the fact that there are now more single fathers in the United States, there has not been a proportionate increase in the amount of literature dealing specifically with these men and the issues that concern them. Moreover, even with the limited amount of information about single fathers, there is markedly less that concerns itself substantially with the African American single father.

African American fathers are usually portrayed as men who feel no parental responsibility toward their children, leaving their partners without any type of support. This is strongly reflected in the published literature about African American fathers. For example, in a major university library computer search of the literature, using black men, black single parents, and black fathers, as search terms, most articles discussed the absent black father, single mothers (Malson and Woody 1985), or adolescent black fathers (Hendricks 1983). Researchers have neglected to study and report the positive story of African American men actively seeking not only monetary but also parental responsibility for their children. The absence of such studies is consistent and supportive of creating a research reality of invisibility for positive black fathers. If all one reads about are the negatives associated with black fathers, a "reality" of merely these negatives is perpetuated. It appears that researchers do not want to study the positive aspects, strategies, and issues related to black men and their parenting roles. This subtle, yet powerful, neglect of the positive fuels the M.E.E.S. factor.

African American men have always been placed in a very precarious and dangerous position in America. From the racist dehumanization of slavery to current policies and practices based on a cornerstone of racism, which perpetuate lack of opportunity and victimization, black men have especially been marked for death, both physically and psychologically. Certain events such as the election of the first African American man as governor in Virginia give some Americans a false sense that racism is on the decline. It also gives one the false hope that anyone who works hard and perseveres will be successful. However, the videotaped, savage beating of Rodney King, an unarmed motorist, by police and their subsequent acquittal take most African Americans back to the cold reality of the persistence of racism and the negative, differential treatment afforded black men in particular. Most African Americans were not shocked by this beating because they, or someone they knew, may have had a similar experience that went unrecorded.

Dr. Noel Cazenave (1981) wrote that all black men in this country are placed in a "double bind." As an ideology we, both men and women of all races, have generally embraced the notion that the man should be the one to "bring home the bacon," provide the economic base. However, the reality is that due to a wide range of variables set into motion and perpetuated by racism, barriers and roadblocks are established to prevent many African American men from playing this economic provider role. Thus, the double bind of being expected to "prove" their manhood through providing the primary economic support of their families and the lack of means to play this role places "manhood" for African American men at risk.

In a capitalistic society "success" is often a result of economics, based on the accumulation of wealth. African Americans, through miseducation, lack of skills and job opportunities, and individual as well as institutional racism, are too frequently blocked in accessing "acceptable" routes of empowerment through economic gain. Data indicate that the economic position of African American men is declining. Although the United States is experiencing the longest economic recovery since World War II, the earnings of young African American men have dropped 30% (U.S. Congress 1989). There seems to be an emergence of a black underclass living in urban ghettos across the nation, which may be a direct result of the inability of African Americans to obtain jobs that provide adequate wages (Wacquant and Wilson 1989). This economic racism and the M.E.E.S. associated with it are not issues that only affect those on the lower end of the economic spectrum. It is also present at the highest levels as evidenced in the Texaco example where a white executive recorded conversations of his peers plotting to destroy files that could possibly prove discrimination toward African Americans. This is the same meeting where these top level executives referred to African Americans as "black jelly beans" and implied that African Americans, like black jelly beans, stick to the bottom of the jar. One is boldly reminded that M.E.E.S. permeates all levels of the economic spectrum. The accumulation of money, made possible by jobs, translates into economic power in America. It is associated with the power to control one's life choices and affect one's circumstances.

Power can also be defined as those who have the privilege of making life-saving and life-giving decisions and follow through on those decisions (Madhubuti 1990). If one accepts this definition, African Americans can be viewed as institutionally powerless in America where such decisions are made predominantly by white men. For example, only one African American firm is represented in the Fortune 500; in 1992, there were no African American senators and only 27 African American men out of the 437 elected to the House of Representatives. Even those who have ascended to the heights of the Senate or House of Representatives complain about being held to a different set of rules, being more scrutinized and less accepted (Congressional Black Caucus Hearings 1992). As indicated by the following news article from *USA Today* (18 March 1995), the fact that an African American man has a very high position does not elevate him above the day-to-day hassles of being black:

> Wilder, the first black elected governor in the USA, told listeners on his weekday radio show on WRVA-AM in Richmond [Virginia] that he was going through a security checkpoint when metal in his suspenders set off a metal detector. While searching him with a hand held magnetrometer, the guard shoved him, Wilder said.
> When Wilder turned to look at the guard's name tag, he charged me and choked me with both hands around my neck and said, "I don't like you. Don't try to get my name," Wilder said.

Although in this same article, Governor Wilder stated that he did not know whether the incident was racially motivated, the fact that he must worry about this is precisely why it is a good indicator of the M.E.E.S. African Americans confront daily. Thus, political power is operationally different for African American men who cannot traverse the country without encountering such micro-aggressions.

In addition to powerlessness and poverty, African American men must also deal with the stereotypes of yesterday and today. The justification used during slavery—that the black man is a beast and must be controlled and broken—has continued. This same image results in such instances as the thousands of lynchings, Scotsboro boys trial, the Tuskegee syphillis experiments, and the Rodney King beating. Many African American men are subjected to the results of the beast image daily as they negotiate their day-to-day livelihood. This beast image has taken a new form in contemporary literature and media. Today the savageness of the African American male is shown through depiction of him primarily as a drug dealer, pimp, drug addict, spouse abuser, gang member, lazy individual thus unemployed, and generally out of control. These images are constantly being reinforced and perpetuated. This is even more so now, with the proliferation of cable channels dishing up their dose of music videos with African American men and boys shown as sexists, drug abusers, and violent and ignorant males. For a young African American man, without adequate education or a sense of empowerment for positive change, these media representations too often become a self-fulfilling prophecy. According to the U.S Department of Health's Task Force on Black and Minority Health Report, in 1983 African Americans constituted 11.5 percent of the population in the United States and 43 percent of all homicide deaths, and black men have a 1:21 lifetime chance of becoming a homicide victim versus 1:131 for white men. Thus, it is not difficult to conclude that the context in which African American men operate is deadly at worst and dangerous at best.

SINGLE FATHERS

Anyone conducting research on African American single fathers will experience silences and voids versus sources. Various on-line databases, such as Melvyl, ERIC, Psyche-Lit, and Dissertation-Abstracts International, generated only two articles that focused on African American single fathers who were not adolescents. These two were found after using the following search terms: African American male, African American fathers, single fathers, black men, black fathers, black parents, and single parenting. The two articles were printed in *Ebony*, not an academic journal but a popular monthly magazine that focuses on African American people in general, and is published by African Americans. I found no articles about African American adult single fathers in the traditional mainstream research literature. Most of the articles concerned with black fathers focus on adolescent fathers (Smith 1988; 269-71) and fathers absent from homes (Sullivan 1989; 48-58).

Despite the lack of information about African American single fathers specifically, there are writings that deal with single fathers in general. "In general" usually means white single fathers in that these studies do not specify an African American sample. Most literature deals with problems that these fathers face, without considering how M.E.E.S. compounds these problems for African American fathers. The topics of research range from difficulty in finding a suitable mate (Littlefield and Keshet 1981) to custody battles for their children (Grief 1985). The single father's ability to take on jobs traditionally thought of as "women's work" such as cooking, cleaning, and child rearing (Greif and Demaris 1990; 259-67), the single father's relationship with the child (Risman and Park 1988; 1049-1063), and the adjustment of the child were also topics of concern to researchers. These issues are also of concern to African American single fathers. However, it is my contention that the process of "fathering" is exacerbated for African American men due to the contextual issues very briefly described in the previous section. Despite the fact that there may currently be minimal empirical mainstream research on African American fathers, the obstacles presented for white men documented in the research not only exist for African American fathers, but are made more difficult by living in an environment where daily micro-aggressions are hurdled at you due to your being black. For example, black fathers share how they must worry that teachers are fearful of their sons due to the prevailing anti-black youth attitudes. These attitudes are based on the depiction of black boys as violent and combative. Black fathers must also constantly worry that their children are exposed to stereotypic images of blacks (i.e., only showing blacks in history lessons regarding slavery or athletic accomplishments, and not including the contributions of black inventors and black professionals). Even with the burden of these micro-agressions and the constant battles faced by black single fathers, many black single men are raising healthy African American children. What follows is a descriptive case study of a small sample of black men who have taken the role of fatherhood very seriously. They represent a segment of the untold story. They are not showcased in popular magazines. They are not in rap videos or featured on the TV news. To me, they represent men like my father who took on the responsibility, doing the best he could with what he had.

CASE STUDY: ANOTHER SIDE OF THE STORY

Methodology/Interview Protocol

Due to the paucity of data collected on single African American fathers in general, and specifically on those who are providing quality care for their children, this study was conceived as a pilot effort. Issues surrounding the perceptions of these fathers — about child rearing, how raising children has affected their lives, their typical day-to-day schedules, and their special needs — were key points of interest. These topics are often addressed among single mothers but not single fathers. Initial discussions with a single fathers' group, combined with information accumulated from the literature search, led to the development of a interview protocol. Most of the questions were open-ended as my goal was to obtain baseline qualitative data from the sample fathers to help in the development of a future survey instrument.

The interview protocol included questions in the following areas:

- Demographics (i.e., age, income)
- Family of orientation (i.e., parents' education, type of household)

- Child(ren) description(s)
- Child-rearing philosophy/practices
- Parenting issues/stress (i.e., how has being a single parent affected lifestyle)

I conducted each interview at a site selected by the fathers: homes, restaurants, and work site lounges. The length of interviews varied from one hour to three hours. The average length was nearly two hours. Sample fathers were open and eager to discuss their situations and share their perspectives. Many shared they had not articulated these issues "out loud" and felt that the discussion was cathartic and extremely helpful.

Methodology/Sample Selection

I live in Oakland, California. Thus, the data sets used for this volume were mainly collected in Oakland. It is a city with a large population of African Americans. It has been touted as the most diverse city in America. In 1991, when the data for this chapter was collected, African American men served as mayor, the newspaper editor, the city manager, and were on the city council and school board. Oakland was also once dubbed the city with the highest murder rate in the state, predominately African American boys and men killing each other. With this wide range of men from which to select, it was not difficult getting a sample of men who take parenting seriously. The major selection criterion was that the father did indeed have full-time or half-time responsibility for parenting. In eight of the ten cases presented in this chapter, the father had at least half-time physical custodial responsibility for his child(ren) as well as financial responsibility.

This study is a pilot intended to generate interest and information on responsible African American single fathers. It is a limited effort and is definitely not all inclusive, neither in scope nor sample. The ten fathers selected for this study were included due to their desire for involvement, ability to discuss and articulate often difficult feelings, ease of access, and the variety of single fathers they represent. These fathers range in age from twenty-four to forty-eight with yearly salaries from $11,000 to $82,000. All of the fathers were employed or in school and stated that without employment it would be difficult if not impossible for them to play the active and responsible father role. Thus, the large category of unemployed men is not included in this sample. This is not to say that men who are unemployed do not take an active parenting role, just that they are not in this data base.

The sample consists of ten case studies. The data will be presented in a descriptive, qualitative case study format with little quantitative data outside of means and modes. An ecological approach of data analysis will be utilized so that the context as well as the content of the interviews can be best understood.

Findings/Sample Description

Due to the exploratory nature of this study, one can better understand the limitations of a small sample, as well as the benefits, if one has a clearer view of the individual cases included. Thus, prior to presenting group data and analyses, brief individual profiles are offered here.

Case # 1

He was born to a military family in 1952. He is currently a counselor at a large university, and a single father of two daughters, ages twenty and ten. He received a bachelors degree and went on to obtain a master's degree. Although his eldest daughter does not currently reside with him, she did for many years, and he still feels a high level of responsibility for both of his daughters. He has been a single parent since 1982, when he separated from the girls' mother.

He expresses concern over the fact that most people consider mothers to be the best parents without giving fathers an equal chance to parent. He believes that if one has basic domestic skills, a financial base, and truly desires to provide, anyone can be a good single parent.

Case # 2

He was born in 1951 to parents who were in real estate. He now works as a sales representative at a major airline, and is a single father of two daughters, ages twenty-one and five. He received a bachelor's degree and attended one year of graduate school in business. He first became a single father when his high school girlfriend became pregnant with their daughter. Although he did not marry or stay with the girlfriend, he assumed responsibility for the child and took custody of her at age seven. He later married another woman and became a father of a second daughter. His wife got involved with drugs and alcohol, and he got divorced. He took custody of their daughter at the time of the divorce. He has been a single father for fifteen years with his oldest daughter, and four years with his youngest.

He states that it is hard to be an African American man in American society because of the terrible situation in which most African American men find themselves. He believes that African Americans need good education and money to compete in this racist society. These commodities are difficult for African American men to attain so they have to really "hustle" to attain success and be strong to handle the resulting stress.

Case # 3

He was born in 1952 and grew up in a single parent household headed by his mother. He is the single father of a son and a daughter, ages thirteen and five. He currently is an administrator at a large university. He received a bachelor's degree in 1974 and a master's degree in 1978. He became a single parent after his divorce, when his son stated that he was unhappy living with his mother. His ex-wife relinquished custody of their son in 1989. He has full custody of his son, and joint custody of his daughter from a second marriage.

He states that he learned a lot about parenting from his mother and is a firm believer in discipline in child rearing. He believes that all children should grow up with two parents. He hopes to be involved in a healthy relationship and that his children will not be single parents when they are older.

Case # 4

He was born in 1946 into a military family, and his parents were divorced when he was twelve. He received a bachelor's degree in 1975 and a master's degree in 1989. He became a single father to his son, age two, when he and his girlfriend, formerly his fiancee, decided not to marry. At the time of this decision they were unaware of her pregnancy. However, after learning of the pregnancy, both agreed that their previous decision not to get married was a sound one and they would both do all they could to provide a happy and healthy environment for their child. He has had half-time custody of his son since his birth in 1990.

He states that it is important to develop effective strategies for marriage. Although he and his fiancee had a terrific relationship, they were not prepared for marriage. He believes in discipline, a strong work ethic, and professes a firm belief in God. He believes that he must be a good role model for his son through both his actions and words.

Case # 5

He was born in 1967 and his parents broke up after his birth. He is currently an undergraduate student at the University of California at Berkeley, and the single father of a five-year old son. He became a single father when he found his son living in a "crack haven" with his ex-girlfriend. He sought and gained physical and legal custody of his son in 1987. He also gained legal custody of his nephew in 1989.

Although his mother died in 1986, he states that he learned a lot from her about parenting; she stressed the importance of finishing school. He says that men feel that they have to be strong and for that reason are less likely to ask for help, but he feels that his hard work is paying off.

Case # 6

He was born in 1955 into a military family and is now a manager of a major telecommunications firm. He obtained a bachelor's degree in 1977 and is the single father of two daughters and one son, ages fifteen, thirteen, and two. He became a single father when his marriage ended in 1986 and he was awarded joint physical and legal custody of his daughters. He and a former girlfriend had an unplanned son in 1989. He pays child support for his son and has liberal visitation rights. He sees his son regularly.

He stresses education with his children and desires to be the best of friends with them because he feels he missed a friendly relationship with his father as a child. He states that girls are harder to raise than boys, but adjustments can be made and anyone can be a good single parent if they work at it and are serious. He is upset that his children are not experiencing the unity of the nuclear black family. He feels that this is important and hopes to one day have this experience.

Case # 7

He was born in 1947 to a middle-class family. He joined the army, went to Viet Nam, and attended some junior college when he returned. He currently works at the Post Office and is the single father of two sons, ages nine and thirteen. He became a single parent in 1979. After his divorce, he noticed that his oldest son had been abused and went to court for custody of the boys. He was given full custody without it being contested.

He believes it is important to listen to others, especially his children. He states that at times he has conflicts with women regarding the time that he spends with his children at their expense. He strives to be a good role model for his two sons and looks forward to the moment when he can feel free—when they are successful young adults.

Case # 8

He was born into a poor family in 1947. He is now a corporate manager for a major H.M.O. He received a bachelor's degree in 1969 and spent two years in law school. He is the single father of two daughters, ages twenty-one and sixteen. He became a single father after his divorce when he had half-time custody of both daughters. His youngest daughter has lived with him since 1986 because she had problems while living with her mother.

He expresses concern over the stereotypes about black men as fathers and feels stress from teachers and counselors when they find out that he is a single father. He expresses a need for special support groups because African American fathers have special problems; consequently, he takes advantage of the counseling services that are offered to him. He is looking forward to a positive and serious relationship and strives to financially and emotionally support his daughters.

Case # 9

He was born in 1944 and is currently a re-entry student in the University of California at Berkeley. He is the single father of a son and a daughter, ages twenty-seven and ten. He became the single parent of his son when his wife died in 1971. He received joint custody of his daughter when he divorced his second wife in 1985. Before becoming a student again, he worked in the private sector in the computer industry.

He has drawn a lot of his parenting skills from his parents and grandparents. He believes in discipline. He stresses the importance of learning about African history and culture and thinks that men can raise children as well as women. He believes that his daughter has made him a more sensitive man, and spends a lot of time with her.

Case # 10

He was born in 1949 into a lower-middle-class family. He received a bachelor's degree in 1972 and obtained an M.B.A. in 1975. He is the single father of a son and a daughter, ages five and nine. He became a single father when he got a divorce in 1990. He has half-time custody of his two children, tries to keep them on the weekends, and sees them frequently during the week. He owns a marketing firm.

At the time of his divorce, his family expressed concern for the children and encouraged him to remain married until his children were in high school. Nonetheless, he and his wife decided to divorce, but they made the transition easier for their children by remaining friendly and explaining to the children that they were not at fault for the divorce. He states that African American fathers have an added stress and seeks some type of support from other African American single fathers.

Findings/Demographics

Table 2.1
Age/Income/Employment/Education

Case No.	Date of Birth	Age at Interview	Annual In- come	Job	Education
1	11/13/52	38	$35,000	Counselor	B.A./M.A.
2	7/21/52	39	$40,000	*Sales Rep.	B.A.
3	8/9/52	38	$52,000	Admin.	B.A./M.A.
4	10/5/46	44	$45,000	Admin.	B.A./M.A.
5	1/4/67	24	$11,200	Work-study	Undergrad.
6	4/13/55	36	$60,000	*Manager	B.S.
7	2/16/47	44	$35,000	Post Office	H.S., some college
8	8/13/47	43	$82,500	*Manager	B.A.
9	1/16/44	48	$72,000•	*Student	Undergrad.
10	8/11/49	42	$50,000	*Marketing	B.S./M.B.A.

* private sector job
• prior to re-entry into school

Table 2.1 shows the key demographic variables of the ten sample fathers. Each father's age, date of birth, income, current employment, and schooling achievements are presented. The average age of the sample was thirty-nine, with an average income of $48,000/year. All of the fathers are middle class, or middle class aspiring. There are two students, one of whom is a re-entry student. Each of the fathers has had post-high school education, with seven having gained college degrees, of whom four went on to achieve post-graduate degrees. Eight of the fathers went directly to college after graduation from high school, and seven of them went to four year colleges.

Data on job trajectory in this sample showed that there was not a direct link between a higher college degree and earning more money on the job. Those who obtained post-graduate degrees (n=4) had an average income of $45,500/year, while those who did not (n=5) had an average income of $56,800/year. However, this is related to the type of employment. Private sector employment proved to be more lucrative than public sector employment. The average income of the five persons employed in the private sector was $60,900/year while the four working in the public sector had average earnings of $41,750/year. Three of the four cases where advanced degrees were earned were employed in the public sector. Thus, the relationship between advanced degrees and income may be mitigated by whether one works in the private or public sector. The work study student was not included in these calculations. There was an average of four previous jobs per case, with a range from one to ten jobs. Length of time on a job is also a likely intervening variable. However, the wide age range and small sample prevent an in-depth exploration of this factor in this study. It is important to note, however, that these fathers had the financial resources to take the role of provider for their children. All fathers now hold white collar jobs.

Table 2.2
Length of Single Parenthood and Level of Responsibility

Case No.	Length of Single Parenthood	Level of Responsibility
1	9 years	Full
2	15 years	Full
3	2 years	Full for son, 25% for daughter
4	1 year	Half
5	4 years	Full
6	5 years	Full
7	12 years	Full
8	9 years	Full
9	7 years	Full
10	3 years	Half

The fathers in the study have had collectively sixty years experience with being single fathers (mean 6.7 years). The range of the length of their parenthood was from one to fifteen years (see table 2.2).

Seven of the fathers have been married to their child(ren)'s mother. This, however, was not a prerequisite for a more positive relationship after the union ended. Of these seven previously married fathers, only one reported a good current relationship, four reported cordial relationships, and two described their relationship as distant. On the other hand, of the three fathers who did not marry the mothers, two indicated good relationships and one reported an excellent relationship (see table 2.3). Circumstances leading to divorce or separation frequently dictate future relationships between the parents. Also length of separation is an important variable to be investigated. For example, nine of the fathers reported tense and stressful relationships with the mothers during the separation process but most have now evolved to a better relationship with their child(ren)'s mother. Fathers also report that family members did not initially think they would follow through and continue their efforts of active parenting, even though their families strongly supported their decision to take custody or maintain strong parental responsibilities.

Table 2.3
Relationship to Mother and Her Family

Case No.	Relationship w/Child(ren)'s Mother	Relationship w/Child(ren)'s Mother's Family
1	Good	None
2*	Cordial	None
3*	Cordial	Cordial
4	Excellent	Excellent
5	Good	Good
6*	Cordial	Good
7*	Distant	Limited
8*	Distant	Limited
9*	Cordial	Good/Excellent
10*	Good	Good

* previously married to mother of child(ren)

Two of the cases (#2 and #5) gained custody due to the mother's drug abuse, one (#7) due to the mother's child abuse, and two (#3 and #8) due to the mother's personal situation not being conducive to the child.

Eight of the fathers still have at least limited contact with the mother's families, with over half of the sample reporting good to excellent relationships.

Findings/Family Background

Family of orientation data refers to the familial background of each father. The data on each father's parents' marital status, parent's education, number of siblings, birth order, family income, and relationship with family is presented in table 2.4. One might assume that people who come from intact families are more likely to stay together in a marriage. However, seven fathers came from intact families. Two fathers have parents who are deceased, but were married up until the time of their deaths. There was one case from a single parent home, headed by his mother. Two cases came from divorced families: one when he was twelve years old; the second, after his birth, however, his mother remarried when he was seven. There was an average number of four to five children per family. Half of the families were classified as poor or working class, earning less that $20,000/year while the other half were classified as middle or upper class, earning more than $20,000/year. In all seven cases where sample fathers grew up in intact families, their fathers were employed. Regarding birth order, six cases were middle children, three were the youngest, and one was the oldest.

Table 2.4
Family of Orientation

Case No.	Parental Marital Status	Parent's Ed. M/F	Siblings	Birth Order*	Family Income•	Familial Relations
1	Married	H.S./A.A.	2	2 (M)	Middle	Excellent
2	Married	H.S./H.S.	4	3 (M)	Upper-Middle	Excellent
3	Single-Mother	H.S./H.S.	2	3 (Y)	Poor	Excellent
4	Divorced	3rd grade/ Self-ed.	8	3 (M)	Working Class	Excellent
5	Divorced	Undergrad. /1 yr. coll.	9	8 (M)	Middle	Good
6	Married	H.S./A.A.	2	3 (Y)	Middle	Excellent
7	Married	B.A./B.A.	2	1 (O)	Middle	Excellent
8	Married	9th grade/ 6th grade	4	5 (Y)	Poor	Good
9	Married	H.S./2nd grade	9	3 (M)	Poor	Excellent
10	Married	6th grade/ 6th grade	5	3 (M)	Working Class	Excellent

* Y = Youngest Child   • Poor = Less than $10,000/yr.

M = Middle Child   Working Class =$10,000−$20,000/yr.

O = Oldest Child   Middle = $20,000−$40,000/yr.

               Upper-Middle = $40,000−$50,000/yr.

It is important to note that *all* fathers interviewed stated that they have good/excellent relationships with their family of orientation and that this relationship of support promoted their fathering role and helped reduce the stresses of day-to-day management of time and energy. Often grandparents, and brothers/sisters would help with child care, transportation, and general emotional support.

Findings/Children's Data

Table 2.5 shows the number of children that each father is caring for, the child(ren)'s gender, and age. There were a total of nineteen children in the study, eleven girls and eight boys, with ages ranging from one to twenty-seven. The average age was twelve years, with a mode of five years (n=4). However, there were also three children that were thirteen years old. There were two fathers with one child, seven fathers with two children, and one father with three children. The average was nearly two children per family.

When asked to describe their child(ren), each father was open and candid. Only two, however, talked of physical qualities such as cute and beautiful. The majority of the fathers concentrated on personality traits. Most descriptions of daughters included characteristics such as sensitive, independent, intelligent, sweet, and strong willed. Descriptions of sons included shy, athletic, intelligent, mischievous, stubborn, aggressive, and well mannered.

Table 2.5
Children's Data

Case No.	Number of Children	Gender	Age
1	2	F, F	20, 10
2	2	F, F	21, 5
3	2	M, F	13, 5
4	1	M	1
5	1	M	5
6	3	F, F, M	15, 13, 2
7	2	M, M	19, 13
8	2	F, F	21, 16
9	2	F, M	10, 27
10	2	M, F	5, 9
	Mean 1.9		Mean 12+ years

Findings/Child-Rearing Philosophy and Future Goals

"Folk" knowledge implies that fathers are more strict than mothers. This common belief is consistent with models that dichotomize the expressive (i.e., affectionate) versus the provider role. Mothers are thought to be the expressive parent, and fathers the provider parent. In African American families these gender-based dichotomies are not as prevalent (Peters 1976) but do exist. Eight of the fathers mentioned discipline when discussing their child-rearing philosophies and practices. Issues such as a "respect for elders" and a need to instill "strong work ethics" were compatible with this theme. Half of the fathers discussed the need to "just provide" for their children. Comments such as "I need to make sure food is on the table" and "I want to give them the best that I can" emphasize the provider role.

Fathers used a variety of methods to follow through on their commitment to discipline. Table 2.6 presents the number of fathers who utilized the methods listed. In addition to the categories of response, one father mentioned yelling; he stated that raising his voice has had a very powerful effect on his children. The vast majority of our fathers prefer to discuss or talk with/to their children; however, six stated that they do spank when they feel it necessary to do so. There was no differentiation according to child's gender in the responses to this question; however, restrictions, isolation, extra chores, and withdrawal of privileges were more common with older children.

These data indicate that perhaps the single African American father is learning the more expressive role through experience. When asked about their methods of affection or positive reinforcement nearly all of them stated that hugs (n=10) and kisses (n=9) are a regular part of their positive reinforcement program. The one father who did not use kissing as a show of his affection (case #5) was our youngest father with a son. However, the other two fathers with only sons did use kissing as a positive reinforcer. Table 2.7 provides data on these and the other methods used.

Table 2.6
Methods of Discipline

Method	# Yes
Extra Chores	4
Spanking	6
Restriction	8
Lecture Child(ren)	9
Early Bed Time	1
Withdraw Privileges	6
Discussion of Problem	8
Isolation in Room	4
Other: Yelling	1

When asked about gender differences in raising children, the most consistent issue was that of grooming (n=4). Girls were perceived as more sensitive (n=4). Developmental differences that lead to fathers' concern about pregnancy also surfaced (n=3). Thus these fathers felt a need to be more protective and strict with their girls. A couple of fathers stated that they knew what was on young boys' minds since they were boys once, and had good reason to be overprotective.

Table 2.7
Methods of Affection/Positive Reinforcement

Method	# Yes
Hugs	10
Give Money	6
Allow to Stay Up Later	2
Extra Privileges	2
Kisses	9
Talk with Child(ren)	9
Take Someplace Special	8
Create a Celebration	3
Other: Surprise Gift, Smile and Laugh,	4
Buy Clothes, Praise in Front of Others	

Girls are more sensitive and more loving, she hugs and kisses a lot. She makes me more sensitive.
    (Case #9)

I try to minimize my own sexism and stereotypic behavior because of my daughter. (Case #10)

Given their perceptions of the activities of young boys, particularly the stereotypes of young African American boys, and their protective feelings regarding their daughters, fathers felt particularly stressed in this area of sexuality. This is mentioned again when fathers report pregnancy and safety as being two of their greatest parenting fears.

Findings/Parenting and M.E.E.S.

I felt that it was important to initially ask fathers about their father role without dealing with race. I asked them what was the most difficult aspect of being a single father. In response, the lack of support was commonly cited. They made statements such as:

The fact that we're not in a traditional family with mom, dad, and child or have the luxury of time shared when two people are together. (Case #4)

Not being able to talk with someone about shared parenting problems — parents can give each other motivation when they are together — now it's all internal. (Case #3)

Sometimes I get frustrated and feel like giving up — there is no one to share my frustrations with. (Case #7)

This feeling of being alone without anyone to share frustrations with or anyone with whom to discuss problems is clearly an issue for most single parents. However, in the case of these fathers, the M.E.E.S. factor plays a burdensome role in their isolation. They share that there are times when they know that people think they are "weekend" only dads because they are "not used to" seeing single fathers take on a full-time parenting role. This is thought to be particularly true of black fathers. Some of the frustrations the fathers shared center around the race issue — how to tell their sons that people will be fearful of them or judge them in a negative way for no reason at all or how to tell their daughters that "Daddy cannot protect them from people who are racist."

Half of the sample also stated that time juggling was extremely difficult. It was hard to meet the demands of the child, job, and personal life. They all felt added stress on their jobs because they are African American men, but realized the necessity of employment because of their responsibilities. One father stated that he felt he was constantly "walking on a tightrope." Others stated their personal lives suffered the most but also that they missed opportunities for career advancement due to the time they needed to spend with their child(ren). Respondents (n=4) also noted that the sheer responsibility of caring for a developing person was overwhelming. The fathers wanted to know that their children would be accepted but were nagged with the thought that others would see the color of their children's skin first. This constant worry is definitely M.E.E.S. The fathers knew that judgments like this would make life harder for their children, and this was a source of anguish and pain.

Part of the sense of being overwhelmed centered on the fathers' perceived inability to translate the concept of racism and monitor the incidents of racism on behalf of their children without hurting their children's development. Fathers worried about this, especially when they were not there to talk to and see their children daily. Both sample fathers who do not have full physical custody of their children indicated how difficult it was not seeing their children on a daily basis: "not waking up and seeing my son everyday" (case #4). Part of "seeing" his son was to see that his son was okay, that no harm in an unwelcoming society came to him that day.

When asked whether they perceived a difference between being an African American single father versus single mother, all respondents agreed that there was a difference. Three were upset that the myth of mother's being the better and most important parent is still pervasive.

There's a certain fallacy about single parenting that needs to be addressed. *Not* all mothers (like not all fathers) can be good single parents. The fallacy is that kids should be with their mothers. Men aren't given equal opportunity to provide as single parents. (Case #1)

Society is set up so that a woman can get more help from more sources for parenting—just because she is a woman. Men have to portray strength and will be less likely to ask for help, although we need it. (Case #5)

I don't like the idea that because the woman is the vessel by which the child comes, she, society, and the legal system automatically assume and confer on her a mystical greater love for her child, greater ability to care for her child and if there is a separation, that the child will experience the greatest amount of harm being away from her rather than the father. I know she loves him and my son could not get greater care, but I also know she doesn't love him more than I do and he gets equal care from me. (Case #4)

Fathers generally agree (n=7) that men are more strict than women. One father shared, "You are a different kind of buffer—fathers are more decisive, mothers are more tolerant" (case #2). However, the experience of single parenting has alerted and alarmed them to the pervasiveness of the negative stereotypes held about black men and the fact that others may perceive them as "unique" or "special." One father stated that he gets more credit than he deserves because he contradicts the widely held stereotype that black men are not good fathers. Another respondent described how black women always treat him kindly because he is the exception to the "irresponsibility rule" regarding black men. Fathers felt that most African American women did accept the stereotypes that put added stress on the men and boys. One father stated the case eloquently:

There are stereotypes about black men as parents that abound, particularly in school when they are faced with counselors and teachers. They are surprised. At times I have had to emphasize things because they were so superficial. They are surprised that you are holding a child up to certain standards and that you don't back down. They just don't expect us to be caring. The media portrays the negative image and they've bought into it. There are few support [groups] or networks for black men who are single fathers. I think there is a need for this type of support group. While we have a lot in common with other single parents, there are unique problems confronting the black man. There are gender differences in how society views and treats us. (Case #8)

The theme of support and special needs that African American single fathers face is repeated throughout many of the interviews. The fact that you have to act as a buffer against the racism or you have to serve as a role model since so few are made visible for black children is a typical response. The notion of identity formation within a society that does not value African Americans was noted as problematic for half the sample.

I've been in both worlds. I think single black men understand that their children have to have a role model. When black kids look at their history, they only see the nega- tive. They think slavery is their culture. I think it is important that black kids be taught, not European history, but African history. They'll see the richness and want to do something. Perhaps we can get them away from the "what is there to live for attitude." (Case #9)

There is also a perception among the fathers that African American children have special needs. Most fathers (n=8) believe that the child must experience unity and family. Many accept their personal decision to divorce but regret that their children are not in an intact family. Helping the child cope with racism and identity issues is a common thread woven into their responses.

Since there is a 50–50 divorce agreement in physical and legal custody, the kids see both parents equally. But, I do believe that there is a major need for them to see the unity in the black family. (Case #6)

Fathers also have fears about being single and raising their children (see ta- ble 2.8). Clearly, the protective mode emerges as most fathers indicate a fear of something unforeseen happening to their children that they cannot control. Liv- ing in a society that does not seem to care whether African American children succeed or fail makes parenting even more difficult according to these fathers. Thus, fathers realize that they cannot control racism but must work to buffer its impact. However, the joys accrued by these fathers are worth the stress of cop- ing with these fears by themselves. Fathers speak with warmth and pride as they describe the many joys of parenting (see table 2.9). Filling the role of father without the support of a live-in mate has both helped and hindered these fathers. When asked specifically about a set of key variables, fathers were more than twice as likely to have a "helped" response versus a "hindered" response (see ta- ble 2.10). Fathers felt that they had to work harder, plan more carefully, and get a better education because they had the responsibility of their child(ren). They also expressed the need to keep a job and not take risks regarding employment because they know that it is harder to get another job if you happen to be black. The majority of the respondents felt that being a single father hindered their upward mobility.

Table 2.8
Fears Among Fathers

Case No.	Fears
1	daughter getting hurt; not excelling in school; pregnancy; inability to perform as a parent
2	something happening to the children
3	kids getting hurt; dying; not coming to him when son needs help
4	conveying the wrong image through actions; failure in preparation for young adulthood; get wrong message about family; son getting hurt
5	failure; making a mistake that affects everyone; walking on a tightrope and falling off
6	pregnancy; not self-sufficient; lack of good education; getting hurt; date rape
7	didn't know how to do things when I first started; fear of something happening to them
8	that my behavior has hindered the kids from reaching their maximum potential
9	no fear for my son; fear of pregnancy
10	how to raise a sensitive, healthy child in a hostile world; whether divorce has negatively affected my daughter

Clearly, the concrete situation with which single fathers must cope, forces more family networking and personal growth (n=10). Dating can often be a problem, as one father observed:

Sometimes I have conflicts with black women regarding sharing my time. I've been told that I was *too* involved with my kids. (Case #7)

Also, the additional financial burden of raising children was experienced by the majority of the sample (n=8). This impediment is reflected not only in their spending money to support their children, but also in the fact that they feel unable to put in the time to facilitate upward mobility on their jobs. Three fathers had goals of completing or going back to school, but felt they would not have the time to do their child-rearing responsibilities if they did. However, most of the fathers (n=6) thought that the parenting experience was in itself educational.

Each father wanted his child to do well, but some had to make personal adjustments. Three men discussed how their fathering role made them decrease alcohol consumption and end drug use. Another spoke of how his self-image was elevated each time he saw his child happy. Undoubtedly, the changes that such experiences yield for the father are not measurable in an interview. Fathers talked about goals for their children in similar ways. Each wanted the child to be healthy, both physically and psychologically. Six spoke specifically about wanting their children to get a good formal education. They realized that as blacks, education would be more important because lack of it would be used to exclude their children from participating fully in society. The stereotype of dumb and uneducable was brought forth by one father who vowed that his child would be educated to help others see that black children are not only educable, but can also excel if given the proper support and guidance.

Table 2.9
Joys of Fathering

Case No.	Joys
1	daily exchange; seeing daughter excel; feeling of accomplishment
2	being a part of their life; the fact that they are happy to see me
3	morning exchanges; daughter saying "Daddy" in a special way; one asking about the other
4	being a father; knowing that my son loves me; ability to care for him; our time together
5	son who cares, loves, and looks up to him; hard work paying off
6	friendship; watching development; teaching athletics; love
7	getting involved; PTA
8	daughter coming back as an adult and telling him how much she appreciates and understands him; before and after look at my daughters
9	just my relationship with the kids; mutual respect; bond of love; thinking the world of each other
10	going out and spending time with them; watching them grow; that I have skills my kids need and I can provide

In describing goals for themselves, fathers had a wide range of responses. Some examples were: to stop smoking; to build a financial base; to no longer be a single parent; to get a Ph.D.; to have the ability to help all of the extended family; to be in good shape and be able to continue enjoying sex until I am eighty years old; to always have a positive relationship with my child; to have better self-knowledge; to have a healthy relationship with a mate. One father pensively reflected on the question, suddenly smiled, and said, "I want to be able to see my children as successful adults, take a deep breath and say, I'm free!"

Table 2.10
Effect of Single Parenthood on Key Variables

Variable	Helped	Hindered	Don't Know/N.A.
Dating	1	5	4
Job Performance	4	2	4
Upward Mobility	2	6	2
Financial Situation	1	8	1
Family Networking	10	0	0
Education	6	3	1
Personal Growth	10	0	0
Planning Behavior	8	1	1
Self-Image	8	1	1
Others' Image of You	9	1	0

SUMMARY/FUTURE DIRECTIONS

Research and articles published on African American fathers would lead one to conclude that there is more interest in their absence and negligence than in their presence and contributions. Living in an environment that ignores your existence and appears not to appreciate you contributes to the mundane extreme environmental stress of black fathers. This does have an impact on the lives of fathers such as those in this sample. It creates the stress of feeling you are always going against societal odds, that you always must be ready to battle the stereotype. One is constantly inundated with a barrage of negative statistics, media images, and news about the problems of African Americans, particularly the African American man. Clearly, this limited pilot study will not have the impact of decades of research based on a pathological model for viewing differences among people. It does, however, present data on fathers rarely depicted—in academic research or in the popular media.

The ten fathers in this case study are each struggling to raise healthy and happy African American children under very difficult circumstances. All of the fathers are employed and have attended classes beyond high school. In a country where the dropout rate for African American boys in junior and senior high school is estimated to be over 30 percent, this commitment does set these fathers apart. In addition, the mere fact that they are taking half- to full-time responsibility for their children distinguishes them from most divorced or separated fathers of *any* race. There are those who might argue that their behavior sets them apart from many fathers in married households! Although these fathers do appear to stand out from the fathers about whom we normally read, they need not be considered "unique" or "rare." It is the intent of this study to explore information on variables and contexts that might help to facilitate the growth of responsible fatherhood. Success, or even attempts at success, should be models for further development. One aspect of M.E.E.S. is that different standards often apply when one focuses on African Americans. Instead of studying success, mainstream America has focused only on failure among African American fathers as indicated by the lack of empirical studies on responsible adult black fathers. Somehow, the case study fathers have been able to hurdle the many barriers confronting single fathers and have, in the process, been able to control the M.E.E.S. factor. Needless to say, each has testified to the difficulty of this task—difficult, yes; insurmountable, no.

All of the case study fathers reported good to excellent relationships with their own family of orientation and seven of them came from intact families. With rising divorce rates and teenage pregnancies, the reexamination of the causes underlying disintegration of core family values is critical. One possible reason emerging from these data is that of employment. In the nine families of orientation where there were fathers present, *each* was employed—even the father with only a second-grade education. As indicated by the work of Cazenave described previously, the notion of manhood, intricately tied into economic ability to provide for families, is an important issue that can be measured by education and employment. Given the national statistics in education and employment, greater effort is mandatory for any measure of success among African American men. A growing technological environment calls for a more educated population. Competing in the labor market with fewer skills because your schooling was inappropriate, through no fault of your own, but because you were in a poor, inner-city school, adds to the M.E.E.S. factor.

"Last hired, first fired," another M.E.E.S. factor scenario, is not just a fictitious notion for African Americans who have disproportionately been employed in the public sector versus private sector due to laws and affirmative action. Even affirmative action is now being challenged in courts across this country. In this sample, the disparity between the public sector and private sector salaries was considerable. It proved to be a greater variable than advanced degrees for income generation. Instead of curtailing and abandoning affirmative action, a greater push to bolster private sector employment and the development of a private sector with the needs of African Americans in the forefront would be conducive to more income power among African American men. Inner-city "enterprise zones," such as those suggested by the Rebuild L.A. Committee after the riots and those that are now being implemented in many urban settings with the objectives of bringing businesses into depressed areas and providing employment opportunities for the residents, make sense conceptually. This type of economic action would enable African American fathers to better perform the provider role or at least have the viable option to do so. Economic empowerment is a key to promoting fatherhood in our communities. It is also an important, and some argue the most important, tool to combat M.E.E.S.

The experiences of the case study fathers also illuminate some of the practical issues that too often have been kept in the dark. Can men be as good at parenting as women? These fathers resent those who feel parenting is a gender-based activity and show that, in their cases, men can do the job when they possess the right attitude and support. With the changing roles in society today, it is evident that much can be learned and much needs to be changed about how we address the custody and parenting rights issues. What qualities make a good parent? Have equal gender rights advancements also created problems that were formerly viewed as "male" problems among women, i.e., drug use, child abuse, and so forth? On the other side of the coin, have advancements in equal gender rights created a more supportive environment for fathers to take their parenting responsibilities more seriously? How does mundane extreme environmental stress affect the dynamics of parenting in black single parent households and the relationships between parents and children in such settings? For example, are fathers less likely to seek custody because of perceptions of racism in employment, in the courts, in social service agencies?

Future research agendas around race, gender, and class differences in these areas, as well as in how parents show and use discipline and affection and prepare their children to face an often unfriendly society, are in order. These fathers, in particular, felt that their experiences have made them more sensitive to the "work of women." Follow-up on the lives of children raised by fathers is also an important area for further research. Most of the fathers discussed their lack of support in the community and the special needs and issues African American fathers face. To fill this void, support services can be developed by social services providers. Finally, investigating the strategies that fathers use to help their children cope with a variety of personal, environmental, and racial issues would be useful—not only for the support groups, but for parents in general.

This pilot study is but a brief glimpse into the African American fathers' experiences and perceptions. Considerably more work must be done to help maximize the potential of good parenting, but also to let our community know that African American men are diverse and complex. All African Americans have to live daily with the unique stresses of being black, the M.E.E.S. factor; however, the triple stress of being a black man, single, and a responsible parent creates a unique set of stress factors. This pilot study indicates that there are those who overcome these barriers successfully by applying strategies that foster their success. It also emphasizes the importance of having the financial means to play the father role. The interplay between fiscal/employment issues and successful strategies for single fathers must be more carefully explored, understood, and transmitted to policy makers.

I salute the fathers in this case study for their perseverance and persistence in fighting the "stereotype." They are not only good fathers but strong African American men on a mission to raise strong, healthy African American children.

Like my father and his father before him, they are negotiating the M.E.E.S. factor and providing successful role models for their children and extended families.

3

The Flip Side of Teen Mothers:
Their Perspectives on Young Fathers

INTRODUCTION

There are scenes in one's life that can be brought forward at will — scenes that are vivid and precise. For example, I don't think I will ever forget that time I left Stanford University for one of my usual visits home to Seaside. My family, parents, and two younger brothers lived in Seaside, a small retirement community adjacent to Fort Ord in northern California. I got home and learned that one of my brothers, a senior in high school, was going to be an unexpected father. I clearly remember being in my room (even now nearly fifty years old, I still claim it as "my room") and my brother, tall and handsome, coming in to speak with me. He had a sheepish, yet defiant, look upon his face. I wasn't sure what to expect, but was truly unprepared to hear what he had to say. He told me that his girlfriend was pregnant and that she was going to have the baby because she didn't want to have an abortion. His girlfriend was a sweet young girl who lived down the street on the next block. A thousand questions entered my mind: How far along was she? Did she really object to abortion or was she afraid? Or was she too far along? What is he going to do about child care? Is this going to affect him going away to college as he planned? Did he plan on marriage? Would she be able to finish high school? However, the only question that was stated out loud was "Have you told Mom and Dad yet?"

Having lived with a father who "blamed" my mother for anything that went wrong with my brothers and me, I was concerned about how he would respond to the news and how my mother would respond (both as a mother and to how my father would respond). My brother said that he hadn't told them yet. A strategy had to be developed. Of course, I wondered why I was the one who was the first in the family to have to hear the news. But then, upon reflection, I felt good that my brother trusted me. I love my brother and would do whatever it took to help. We talked about how this should be handled. We came to the conclusion that we should tell my dad the news first. I rationalized that my dad always felt he was left out of our lives since he was at work all of the time and he really wasn't the "warm and fuzzy" kind of father one could open up to. However, he was always responsible. We knew he cared, but he had a strange way of show-ing it. We told him. He was sad and disappointed, but I know he was glad we told him first. My mom was really upset. I'm sure she cried a lot. But ulti-mately, the family came to grips with the fact that we would now be grandpar-ents, fathers, aunties, and uncles. My beautiful niece was born in December of that year. My mom baby-sat for my niece while her mother finished her last year and a half of high school. I took my brother to live with me at Stanford that summer, and he got a job at Marine World. He never married my niece's mother but took responsibility for my niece the best way he could. He went on to college and graduated. Currently all are doing well. His daughter finished high school and is now a happily married mother. She has a positive relation-ship with her husband, an African American man. Ironically, her husband has taken on the paternal responsibility of three of his nieces and nephews. We had a fairly happy ending. However, this is not always the case with young teen mothers and fathers.

Chapter 2 highlighted employed black men who took the full responsibility of fatherhood. This chapter visits a group of young women who were not as fortunate. They had children as teenagers, and the fathers of their babies were not college educated or successfully employed. Instead of having the triple stress of being black, male, and a single parent mitigated by education and employment, these young teens are stressed because of being black, teenaged, and a single par-ent without the advantage of having a good education or being successfully em-ployed. Being a teen mother is a difficult undertaking for anyone. It is neither socially acceptable nor desirable. However, the existence of stereotypes depict-ing black women as being "property" and sexually permissive helps create an environment where these teen mothers are seen as being totally at fault for their "indiscretions."

Unfortunately social and structural factors—such as the education and wel-fare system, residence options, hope and trust in the future, to name just a few—do not intervene on behalf of these mothers in their day-to-day interactions with the world. Quite the contrary, they are subjected to stresses because of their motherhood as well as M.E.E.S. There is a strong likelihood that the M.E.E.S. factor had a strong effect on these adolescents before they became teen mothers. This may have even been a critical aspect leading to their becoming teen moth-ers. In this chapter a brief overview of the plight of black teen mothers is pro-vided as the backdrop for our understanding of the sample teen mothers, who share some of their perspectives regarding how they cope with their situation.

BACKGROUND

According to census data, in 1992 African American teens led the country in births, with 120 births per 1,000 African American females between the ages of eleven and nineteen. The external and internal home environment, level of edu-cation, and main focus of support upon which teenagers have to rely have often been identified as determinants of teenage pregnancy.

Slavery and the subsequent centuries of inequity have forced black children to bear a disproportionate share of the burden of poverty and economic decline in America. They are at substantially higher risk than white children for experiencing an array of socioemotional and medical problems (McLloyd and Flanagan 1990). Nearly two-thirds of all black children are born to teenage mothers. This number becomes even more frightening when one considers that 22 percent of all black males between the ages of twenty and twenty-nine (the typical age of the fathers of these babies) are in jail or under court supervision. According to researchers, the major factors contributing to the circumstances affecting urban black children and teens are lower levels of education, higher rates of unemployment, low wages, and higher levels of marital discord (Grief 1985; Coner-Edwards and Spurlock 1988; Hacker 1992). I believe that the higher levels of marital discord result from the lack of employment and education and should be viewed as a byproduct versus a cause. Nonetheless, this means that an alarming number of black children are born into at-risk environments. Inexperienced mothers, absent fathers, and poverty do not make for positive child-rearing circumstances. Such environments create barriers for the fostering of children who are able to compete in a technologically advanced society. Such statistics do not generally result in "happy endings" as was the case with my brother and niece. They had support. Too often, the type of support necessary, first to avoid the increase of teen mother- and fatherhood, and then to foster positive outcomes for those who do have these children, is not available. This set of circumstances has a very deleterious effect on many of our young people. Understanding their perceptions and how they cope with the stresses inherent in being teen parents is a starting point for making an impact on their lives and the lives of their children.

Our young people are disproportionately affected by multi-generational poverty and under- or mis-education and frequently do not feel they can seize an opportunity to break the cycle of poverty (Edelman 1993). In addition, the plight of our children is exacerbated by the images projected in a society that has repeatedly shown them that black children are not a high priority. Black youths are growing up in a "uniquely oppressive environment" because of limited opportunity for economic or social advancement and the hostility of those who appear to control their environments. The absence of traditional "rites of passage" into puberty with community direction and support, coupled with the ongoing media blitz on the joys of sexuality, entice young black boys and girls to engage in sex without thought to future consequences. The negative stereotype of African American youth by the press adds to the deterioration of self-worth, as described previously, and is a major contributing factor to mundane extreme environmental stress.

Teen pregnancy is just one of the many complications of a society that is cursed with racism, a growing number of impoverished citizens, and a failing public educational system. The effects of all these social and structural circumstances is compounded by M.E.E.S., thus leading to a higher level and intensity of stress among black families (Peters and Massey 1983). We are more likely to be economically disadvantaged, undereducated, and socially disenfranchised because of the aforementioned circumstances. Recent studies have found that race differences regarding stress were consistently and markedly greater among those with low incomes than among those with higher ones. Researchers found that the true effect of race is suppressed, and the true effect of social class is magnified, in models that fail to take the interaction of race and social class into consideration (McLloyd and Flanagan 1990). Many of these stress and class factors have been discussed vis-à-vis adults. Very little mention is given to looking at the interaction of these variables among teenagers, particularly African American teenagers.

The popular attention given to teenage pregnancy in public heath, social welfare, and mainstream literature is overwhelming. The continued increase in adolescent and teenage pregnancy has resulted in an enormous amount of research and study on this topic. Using the University of California at Berkeley's computer database, 142 listings were obtained on teenage pregnancy. Of the 142 listings, 11.3 percent (n=16) dealt specifically with issues pertaining to African American teens. Of these, one-third (n=5) focused on the relationship or absence of black teenage fathers in regard to the mother of their babies and/or their children. Another third (n=5) studied the rise of urban teenage birthrates and other abstract society effects. The remaining six researched support systems and birth alternatives, and offered comparisons of different populations of pregnant teens and adults. As evidenced by these articles, the issues surrounding African American youth were not totally ignored. This, if you recall from the last chapter, is in contrast to no articles on responsible black fathers in the mainstream literature. However, the attention given African American teens is relatively little and focuses on the researchers' perceptions and paradigms, not the perceptions, paradigms, and perspectives of the black teens. This is particularly true regarding black teen fathers. This chapter only partially addresses this gap. The mothers' perceptions of the fathers of their babies are the data source and are an important starting point for understanding how these contextual issues impact the day-to-day thoughts and functioning of this teenage parent population.

CONTEXT OF STUDY

The data collection for this chapter represents a collaborative effort among three programs that provide services to teen parents. The data were collected in Oakland, California, where, like in many inner cities, teen pregnancy is considered to be at epidemic proportions in the city's lower-income black communities. The city has a population of approximately 400,000 people. According to the 1990 census, over 60 percent of this population is made up of ethnic minorities, with the majority of these being black. The percentages of blacks and other minorities have increased over the past decade. Although growing in many positive directions, Oakland embodies many problems associated with "inner cities": low income, high crime rates, white flight to neighboring suburbs, schools with test scores below the national levels, and increasing drug and substance abuse. The average black income is approximately $12,000 and one-quarter of black families have incomes below the poverty level (U.S. Census 1986). The official city-wide unemployment rate is close to 10 percent. However, the rate for black teens is thought to be closer to 40 percent.

In addition to unemployment, the issues surrounding adolescence are compounded by parenthood. However, due to limited resources and opportunities available to poor African American youth and families, their lives are unfolding within a uniquely oppressive environment. Dr. Chester Pierce (1969) compared this situation of continuing, subliminal stressful conditions in the lives of black families in America to the isolation and stress of Eskimos in the Arctic and extreme, exotic environment, that is, an environment where racism and subtle oppression are ubiquitous, constant, continuing, and mundane. As mentioned in previous chapters, Pierce suggested that this presents many psychosocial difficulties and stresses for blacks in general. Black teen parents are coping with this mundane extreme stress while simultaneously combating the negative stigmas and consequences of adolescent parenthood. This all happens developmentally at the time when they, like all teens, must grapple with what one must to do become an "adult."

Black teen fathers also carry a tremendous burden—they are black, they are adolescents, they are male, and they are all unprepared fathers. The double bind Dr. Noel Cazanave (1981) described which was presented in the previous chapter, is truly in effect for these young teens. The reality is that many black men, particularly teens, cannot enact the provider role, thought to be essential for manhood in this society. Thus, the double bind of being expected to "prove" their manhood through providing the economic support of their new babies and the lack of means to play this role is a real problem for young teen fathers who are at the highest levels of unemployment in this country. In some communities the rate is over 50 percent!

Cazenave (1981) also described how black men creatively adapt to this situation, mainly by engaging in a "macho" role—as the tough guy with his sexual conquests and dominating behaviors. Young boys in lower-class communities see these behaviors and emulate them, often without the contrast of more positive role models to serve as buffers and interpreters of the environment. For example, sexual behavior is considered a cornerstone of masculinity. Young boys frequently choose early sexual behavior to prove their masculinity. Past research in the area of onset of sexual interaction indicates black boys engage in sexual activity earlier as a result of blockages in the opportunity structure in our society (Broderick 1965; Staples 1985). There is great pressure to prove oneself and one's masculinity when one is unemployed and sees no real future in the traditional occupational hierarchy. Each of these factors contributes to the large numbers of teen births in cities such as Oakland.

Clearly, we as adults have not been successful in providing the necessary programs to effectively make a large difference in the lives of these teenagers. We have had individual success stories, but not the large group successes that change the statistics. Listening to teen parents is one way to examine these issues from their perspectives and vantage points. Perhaps, it is one method of gaining insights into ways that can make a collective difference.

DATA COLLECTION

Fifty teen mothers, including eight mothers-to-be, completed a two-page questionnaire about their education, living and job status, and the fathers of their babies. The questionnaire also covered issues regarding the relationship each respondent had with the baby's father, her current needs, and her perception of the role played by the baby's father. The questionnaires were administered one-on-one or in small groups with a staff member from a nonprofit organization that housed a program focused on support of teen mothers. In addition to the questionnaire, focus groups about the issues on the questionnaire were held with three groups of respondents. All respondents were involved in at least one program focusing on teen mothers. The sample represents young mothers who are more connected with services than are many other teen mothers. These sample mothers may be less isolated, and perhaps more motivated to reach out for help.

FINDINGS/DEMOGRAPHICS

The questionnaire respondents (n=50) ranged in age between fourteen and twenty-one with the majority (74%) being between fifteen and seventeen years old. At the birth of their babies, the mothers ages ranged between twelve and nineteen years old with 90 percent being seventeen and younger. The fathers were older, with an age range from thirteen to twenty-seven years at the birth of their children. However, the majority (60%) of the fathers were between seventeen and nineteen years old. Thus, the fathers generally were a couple of years older than the teen mothers.

Most teen mothers and fathers lived with their mothers at the time of their babies' births—68 percent of teen mothers and 54 percent of the teen fathers. When you included living within a kinship network, the numbers increased to 86 percent for both teen fathers and mothers. Thus the strong kinship patterns and the extended family that have traditionally characterized black families was still the norm for our sample.

Regarding education, 4 percent of our responding teen mothers had graduated from high school at the time of their babies' births. Twenty-eight percent of the fathers were high school graduates. On the other hand, 12 percent of the mothers and 32 percent of the fathers had dropped out. Seven (14%) of these fathers had dropped out by the time they were eighteen. The remainder were still in junior or senior high school at the time of the babies' births.

Although there were eight respondents who did not know their babies' fathers' employment situations at the time of their babies births, approximately one-third of the fathers were unemployed (33%), one-third worked part time (24%) or full time (7%), and one-third (36%) were still in school without employment. Thus, the vast majority of these teen fathers were not prepared financially to support their babies, although a third (32%) of the respondents indicated that the fathers of their babies were looking for jobs at the time of the babies' births. Consequently, thirty of the forty-two teen mothers (71%), excluding the pregnant teens (n=8), were receiving Aid to Families with Dependent Children (AFDC) to support their children. Of the remaining twelve mothers, eleven were supported by their families and one by the baby's father.

FATHERS' PARTICIPATION

When we look at the teen mothers' perception of father involvement, we find that fathers do participate on varying levels with their babies. Twenty-four (57%) of the teen mothers reported that the fathers were with them at the hospital during birth and thirty-one (74%) stated that the fathers visited them in the hospital after the birth.

Approximately two-thirds (67%) of the mothers stated that the fathers visit their babies regularly and that they (65%) presently have good relations with the fathers. This may be a sampling artifact since our sample involves very young children, with the majority of the babies (76%) under three years old. Drs. Ewer and Gibbs (1975) found that the relationship between adolescent black mothers and the fathers of their babies change character between conception and the nine months to birth. Typically, the couple sees less and less of one another. In this sample, group discussions with the mothers support findings that many teen fathers tend to become less involved as their children get older and the couples go their separate ways. A variety of reasons for this can be posited. The age of these young parents, the lack of success in employment the fathers may be feeling, their lack of ability to successfully provide for the babies, their lack of a life direction, their inability to maintain a positive relationship with the grandparents of the babies, these are but a few of the reasons these young mothers discussed as to why they are not together with the babies' fathers.

However, these are good indications that these young fathers are generally not denying paternity even though they are not able to take full financial responsibility for the babies. Quite to the contrary, 58 percent of our mothers report receiving some marginal financial support from the fathers, 41 percent report receiving help with baby-sitting, and 84 percent report having good relationships with the father's family.

CONTEXTUAL ISSUES

In an attempt to get a general picture of the fathers, we inquired not only about their demographics and participation with the babies, but also about their involvement with the so-called street culture. Sexual conquest was combined with being violent and tough in Cazenave's (1981) depiction of black men who were caught in the "double bind." Due to the sensitive nature of such issues, we thought there might be hesitancy in reporting physical violence and drug involvement by our teen mothers. However, four (8%) of our sample did respond that their babies' fathers got physically violent and abusive with them. Three did not respond to this question. Nine respondents (18%) stated that the fathers used drugs; seven (14%) stated that the fathers sold drugs; and eleven (22%) stated that the fathers lived with people who sell or use drugs. In the self-reports two of our mothers stated they use drugs and now live with people who use or sell drugs.

In an early survey of 421 teenage boys, 72 percent indicated that they had not used any form of contraception in their last sexual encounter (Finkel and Finkel 1978). Our data indicate that things have not changed much over the past two decades. Our data are consistent with these findings despite the AIDS epidemic surrounding our sample. Slightly over 70 percent of the respondents state the fathers do not use contraceptives. However, over half (52%) state they, the mothers, now use contraceptives. Repeat pregnancies are common occurrences with teen mothers. The discussions indicate that the fathers do not want them to get abortions. This is consistent with Hendricks's (1983) data on unmarried black adolescent fathers. He reports that although there may be a willingness to share contraceptive responsibility, the majority of the fathers surveyed were opposed to abortions.

Researchers have found "a strong sentiment against abortion" on the part of black teens (Hale and Vadies 1977). There is also a belief on the part of black males that contraceptive responsibility should be placed with the female. These sentiments, coupled with the vast amount of misinformation teens have about various birth control methods, ensure future pregnancies. For example, in one group discussion the following statements were made:

- Pills make you get cancer.
- Diaphragms can get knocked around; they move and don't work.
- Pills don't work; you get pregnant on them so why use them?
- My boyfriend thinks condoms are a waste of time and he can't feel it if he uses one.

Many of the comments made in the discussion/focus groups were surprising to the facilitators. Particularly surprising were the positive results from the mother' subjective ratings of the fathers. Several factors would lead one to assume that these teen mothers would not think so positively of the fathers: the mothers were on welfare; the young men had dropped out of school, were unemployed, and were involved with drugs. The following findings are from our mothers' more subjective responses on a listing of descriptors to the question, "Overall, how would you rate your baby's father on ____?" A five-point response scale from excellent to very poor was used.   Excellent and good were combined to yield the following:

- 52 percent felt their babies' fathers were good or excellent fathers.
- 60 percent felt their babies' fathers were good or excellent friends to them.
- 45 percent felt their babies' fathers were good or excellent providers.
- 46 percent felt their babies' fathers were good or excellent role models.
- 46 percent responded that their babies' fathers rated good or excellent as responsible persons.
- 54 percent responded that their babies' fathers rated good or excellent at being loving and affectionate.
- 38 percent rated their babies' fathers good or excellent workers.
- 40 percent rated their babies' fathers good or excellent students.

These subjective ratings almost seem inconsistent with the more specific demographic data presented previously. However, if we look closely at the context of the subjective ratings, we find the concept of "relativity" at work. Gardner Murphy (1947), in his analysis of personality, stated that choice of referents "becomes a wish fulfilling, purposeful mechanism [by which] the individual enhances and defends the self by an appropriate choice of those with whom to identify." Most of our respondents live in environments where many girls become pregnant and have babies. Many of the fathers do not give support. Fathers who pay a little are considered "good" providers—good compared to the referent group of fathers who pay nothing. Possibly this also allows them to defend their own behavior for actually having sex and children by young men who cannot provide adequate support.   Teenagers are really very peer conscious. Many feel and give into the pressure of having sex and babies because they lack the education, self-confidence, and support to say no. Many of our mothers did not see alternative lifestyles as being realistic for them. Many studies in urban school settings report this same peer and relativity process at work for students who get poor grades, but who believe they are average students (St. John 1971; Ogbu 1974; Massey 1975). If the perception is that everyone else in my school is getting poor grades, then students with "C" and "D" grades are indeed average for this school and deemed okay. Similarly, if my friends are having babies and are doing fine, why shouldn't I? Teens want to "fit in" and be like their peers.

TYPOLOGY OF FATHERS

After lengthy individual and group discussions with the sample teen mothers, a typology of fathers emerged:

- Type 1 depicted the teen father who felt very confused about the news of pending paternity. He was going through the typical adolescent search for identity and this news was viewed with great ambivalence. He knew he wasn't prepared. He felt guilty and ashamed but also responsible. He accepted his paternity and tried to lend support but often was not even in the position of supporting himself. He was typically still in school. He felt stressed and guilty.

- Type 2 father reacted quite differently. Although he, too, could not support a child, he was extremely proud of the fact that he was going to be a father. He would typically plead with the pregnant teen not to even consider an abortion. A child represented a symbol of manhood, a source of pride. He fit with Cazenave's (1981) depiction of a young man needing to prove his manhood with few avenues other than sexual conquest with which to do so. In some cases he had one or more children and boasted of his virility. When convenient, he would participate with his child and/or the mother.

- Type 3 represented the father who avoided all the responsibility of his baby. He would go as far as to say the baby wasn't his. Other typical accusations focused on the mother (i.e., "She could have had an abortion"; "She didn't have to say yes", or "She should have used birth control"). He clearly could not face up to the responsibility.

- Type 4 fathers were those young men who really took full legal and financial responsibility for their children. Some were with the teen mother and baby and provided a full-time father figure. Others sent money for support and responded to the needs as they arose even though they were no longer involved with the mother. These fathers were generally older and employed or had the support of their families.

The preceding father types are not fixed positions. Based on group discussions, mothers indicate fathers can move from one type to another just as Schultz (1986) described in his depiction of boyfriends. Other fathers may embody characteristics of more than one of these types at the same time. Nonetheless, each of these father types experienced some form of stress—whether it was from his knowledge that he could not care for his child, his having to depend on others for support, or his dealing with his avoidance of responsibility. I am not suggesting that all teen fathers do not have to cope with these stresses. I am only suggesting that African American teen fathers are also coping with a society that expects them to "mess up," expects them to be irresponsible and does very little to prepare them for such responsibility or provide viable options. They daily face these low expectations and micro-agressions and often do not see a way out, a way to prove their worthiness. The fathers described in the previous chapter had educations and jobs to prove worthiness, as do most of the fathers who typically fit into the Type 4 category.

A few researchers and practicioners have suggested that violence and drugs are part of a death wish of these young black teens who do not see the future as full of promises for them. Broken promises are more the norm for many of these young people. Thus, the M.E.E.S. factor takes on a special significance for these young fathers and mothers. They are grappling with the typical eustress of growing up as well as the distress of growing up black with a child.

SUMMARY/DISCUSSION

These data were collected to get a perspective on young black fathers from the teen mothers, to look at the "flip side" of the coin on teenage pregnancy. Unfortunately, as with many research endeavors, the accessibility of any given sample increases their likelihood of being studied. Consequently, due to both time and fiscal constraints, the perspectives of only the more accessible teen mothers are captured in these data. This interjection is not made to invalidate nor apologize for the data; quite the contrary, the mothers' responses are very informative and provide a lot of insight. However, future research and work with fathers are critical, as indicated by the following summary of findings:

1. The babies' fathers are more likely to be older teens or in their early twenties.
2. Teen parents generally live with their own parent(s) or with relatives.
3. One-third of the fathers had dropped out of school by the time they were eighteen years old.
4. Teen mothers and teen fathers are not prepared for parenthood. It was not planned but it was not actively avoided.
5. Young fathers do participate in the lives of their babies by visiting the baby, baby-sitting, and when possible, providing modest financial help.
6. Contraceptives are not being used by large numbers of sexually active teens.
7. Teen mothers believe their babies' fathers are positive figures despite their inability to fully support their children.
8. When describing their own situation, mothers frequently use teen parents in their environment as their primary reference group when subjectively rating the role of fathers and themselves.
9. Teen fathers are not all alike. Like black families, they are not monolithic. They engage in a wide variety of behaviors regarding their paternity status, some of which are constructive and others detrimental.

Many of these findings validate previous findings and hypotheses regarding teen parenthood. However, an academic, research, or moralistic approach will not begin to solve the multiple problems encountered by our teen parents. A thorough understanding that teen pregnancy, both from the mothers' and fathers' sides of the coin, is merely a symptom of much larger structural, socioeconomic, and political problems is mandatory in any attempt to produce constructive change. Young people do not come into this world with a "worldview" on how things work in this society. It is learned. They are exposed daily to occurrences of overt and covert racism. They are not blind to the inequities brought about by their skin color: being stopped by police for no reason, being ignored by teachers, being looked down on by social service providers, constantly seeing your image projected in a very demeaning fashion. These micro-aggressions are particularly hurtful and damaging to our young people who are trying desperately to come to grips with their identity and sense of worth in a society that still subscribes to the "Black = Bad" equation. In order to provide programs and environments of success for these teen parents, one must consider these societal factors from the vantage points of these teens. One has to recognize that M.E.E.S. is operational in not only adults but also in our young. The next chapter describes just how young some children are when these processes begin to have an effect. This recognition of the daily stress due to one's blackness is not made to blame racism for such problems (although blame is there). Rather, it is to include the awareness and analysis of the manifestations of racism in solutions for reducing the impact of M.E.E.S., so that we can better prepare our young people to cope with it. We cannot pretend that race does not matter. Our children know that it does.

Due to the interconnectedness of the problem, any solution will be also interdependent. The fragmented approach of giving only child care, or only summer jobs, or only training programs will not be sufficient. Any successful program must include the awareness of the context of the problems, plus the perspectives of the young men and young women targeted for intervention. Our youth, our boys and girls, have to be lured away from the "live just for now" orientation and made to really believe they have a positive, worthwhile stake in their future and a firm commitment to our collective future as a cultural/ethnic group and as a multicultural-ethnic society. They will only believe this when we stop attempting to delude them and begin telling them the truth about why African American youth are in the position they are in, and provide them with empowering mechanisms for change.

4

Parenting: Mothers, Magic, M.E.E.S., and Myths

INTRODUCTION

I was told each day that I was brilliant, wonderful, beautiful, special, extraordinary. My mom thought the sun rose and fell above my head. No one could tell her that I was not the picture of perfection. When I cried, she was there to comfort me. When I felt sad, she cheered me up. When I was sick, she nursed me back to health. When I was perplexed, she helped me find my answers. I never needed an alarm clock throughout my stay at home. My mom would come into my room each morning before school and gently rub my back. In a soothing voice, she would say, "It's time to get up and go to school." I knew that by the time I washed up and got dressed, like magic, breakfast would be waiting for me on the table in a spotless dining room. She would sit with me while I ate, or would be in the kitchen fixing my lunch, and ask me what I wanted for dinner. I knew her love was unconditional, unwavering, and at times, I confess my fear, unwarranted.

My mom also has a peculiar sensitivity to the notion of family. Although my father was an army cook and she was unemployed, at home raising three kids, she would always say how wealthy we were, how lucky my brothers and I were to be healthy, have each other, and be part of a loving family. In her own way, by deeds and words, she taught us to share with one another, enjoy one another, and protect one another. She taught us that our family was the cornerstone of our well-being. Thus, family had to be nurtured and always valued. We never had a baby-sitter. Although my mom was friendly and congenial to non-family members, she did not trust her most precious valuables, Alan, Nathan, and I, with other mortals. She was sure, however, that we all had guardian angels and other miscellaneous spiritual protectors. Of course this made sense, why else would we be so perfect?

I knew, however, I was nowhere near perfect. But I also knew that my mom thought I was pretty damn close. That knowledge, coupled by being enveloped by the love of my family, steered me away from doing anything *too* wrong. I knew how disappointed my mom would be. I knew how much she trusted me. I knew how much faith she had in me. I knew, beyond any doubt, that she wanted me to be good, honest, and upstanding. She was always in my corner cheering me on to "make it." Even now with divorce, a mouth too often filled with foul language, and bad credit in my portfolio, my mom still will tell others that she has a perfect daughter.

When my son and daughter were born, I wanted them to feel just like I did when I was young. I didn't take into account that I would get a divorce when my children were two and four years old; that I was a "working woman"; that I would have to daily juggle the roles of mother, father, provider, and nurturer. I really didn't want, nor did I feel equipped, to both "bring home the bacon and stir it up in the pan." My guilt was overwhelming. There were times I felt that I just couldn't do it, that I really didn't know what "it" was. Being a parent was clearly more than I had bargained for. Breakfast did not magically appear each morning. Twitching my nose did not clean the house as it did with Samantha on "Bewitched." Somehow my guardian angel did not send a direct deposit monthly to cover my bills. The responsibility and the reality of parenthood were truly being felt. I tried to extract the things my mom did that made me feel so very special, and do as much as I could to replicate and schedule in those fondly remembered activities, words, and even nonverbal signs and nuances. I was never sure, however, if any of my efforts were sufficient.

My mom never did tell me that being black would create even more fears and insecurities in my continuing attempts to be a good parent. I knew I wasn't alone because I discussed many of my frustrations with peers who also worried about the best route to take in promoting and fostering healthy (mentally as well as physically) black children in a society that too readily devalued them. My esteemed colleague and friend, Dr. Margaret Beale Spencer (Spencer, Brookins, and Allen 1985) has conducted research that led her to the conclusion that many black parents do not consciously prepare their children for positive racial identification. Is this an oversight? Is this merely a strategy black parents use to avoid the pain that discussions of race bring to the table? My quest for child-rearing answers led me to participate in a major research project on parenting of black children.

In 1978, Dr. Jean Carew, principal investigator, in collaboration with Dr. Marie Peters and myself as co-principal investigators, launched a small three-year descriptive study of young black toddlers and infants, appropriately named TIES, an acronym for Toddler and Infant Experiences Study. We were each excited about the prospect of doing a longitudinal observational study from a multidisciplinary approach. Jean, a psychologist, had invested a decade in her observation instrument and was both challenged and fascinated by the new technology that allowed us to capture and store the behavior of children on videotape. Marie, a black family specialist, courageous and unswerving in her ongoing battle with cancer, was equally adamant in her desire to challenge the too frequently perpetuated myth that black children were like Topsey, "they just grew." My work in education and sociology, plus my dive into parenthood, led me to see this as a great opportunity to open an office; where black children were thought to be bright and beautiful; where their parents could have a voice and where I could learn more about parenting. We were all idealistic in thinking that this small study would make a positive difference in how black children and their families were viewed. These ideals, however, motivated us and served to bond us together.

During the course of developing the study, recruiting the families and staff, and opening an office in downtown Oakland, Jean, Marie, and I developed intimate friendships with one another. Professional and personal successes and problems were shared. We used each other as sounding boards for ideas. We rarely agreed about anything! Each of us was known for pushing our own point of view. However, our evolving perspectives, due to our listening to and respect for each other, led to a more healthy, more informed research team. Thus, TIES, which originally was only concerned with toddler and infant experiences, became a symbol of our own personal ties to the project, our cases, our staff, our ideas, and each other.

My respect for my two colleagues grew. They nurtured my professional growth and served as the mentors and role models I had sorely missed in my Stanford graduate experience. I never had an African American female professor throughout my eight years in college and graduate school. My colleagues supported my desire not to have to choose between academia and community service. They provided for me a safe and sturdy bridge between the two. Then this wonderful, magical spell was broken. The hurricanes came and my bridge was to be irreparably damaged. Jean died in her sleep after a serious case of manic depression in the summer of 1981. This was to be our writing year. Marie, who attacked her cancer as she did her life, with vigor and optimism, succumbed to it in the winter of 1982.

The data presented in this chapter represent a small segment of the unreported final interviews, focusing on issues of black parenting, with the TIES sample mothers. They also represent much of what I have learned about parenting over the past decade. Marie and I completed these interviews shortly before her death. I dedicate this work to both she and Jean without whom TIES would have only been a pipe dream. Although the data set may seem old, collected in 1981, it is clearly not dated because the responses and perspectives of the sample parents are still very much relevant and insightful. I hear the same questions, issues, concerns, and responses today when I conduct parenting seminars.

TIES: BLACK MOTHERS' VOICES

Methodology/Sample

Between 1979 and 1981, our TIES research team collected detailed observational and interview data on how black families rear their young children. The TIES project was a broad-gauged, longitudinal investigation of the everyday experiences and development of toddlers. It was also significant because of its inventive methodology. These innovations included special procedures for videotaping toddlers under naturalistic conditions in ordinary home environments; a longitudinal video data bank; a behavior scoring system designed for both eyewitness and video coding; caregiver interviews thematically linked to the video data; and videotaping of widely used tests for toddlers.

In its basic design, conceptualization, and naturalistic observational methodology, the child development and child-rearing component of TIES was built largely on previous work by Carew (1976). The adult interview component of this research, upon which this chapter is based, draws on the previous work of my colleagues and consultants on this project (Carew and Lightfoot 1979; Peters and Massey 1983; McAdoo 1980; Pierce 1969, 1975). Participants were paid for their time at the end of each visit. Although the data in this chapter are merely a small fraction of the three years of data collected in TIES, the context of the data and data collection are important. It will give the reader a feel for how close the researchers and families became over the course of the study. This is unlike the more typical "researcher as an outsider" with pure "objectivity" model. The interviews from which these data were drawn are extracted from the final caregiver interviews of the study. The interviewers, Marie Peters and myself, had already interacted with the caregivers monthly for over two years. Thus, trust had been established and the interviewees were extremely open and straightforward in their responses. To provide a context for the data presentation, the specific objectives of TIES are presented:

- To document and trace longitudinally from age one to four, the daily experiences (behaviors, interactions, activities) of black children, including both the experiences that the child generates for himself/herself in their independent pursuits and those in which their caregiver and others in the family play some part
- To document and trace the course of development of major socioemotional, intellectual, language, creative, self-care, and physical competencies among black children
- To examine the connection between the child's daily experiences (both self-generated and environmentally produced) and their development of the competencies referred to, using three types of assessments: the first based on video-taped observations of the child in the home, the second on caregiver reports, and the third on performance in a standardized test situation
- To document and trace the child-rearing practices and styles used by black caregivers in socializing their infant-toddlers and to identify the underlying rationales, life experiences, life conditions, and personal characteristics that influence these practices and their associated attitudes and expectations
- To document and describe the lives of black families from their own perspectives, focusing on (1) factors that commonly cause stress for black mothers and influence their ability to cope with the problems of parenthood and living in a society in which racial and social discrimination are pervasive aspects of daily life; and (2) sources of happiness, satisfaction, self-esteem, hope, and pride.

Recruitment of families posed a unique set of problems. The target population consisted of black infants and toddlers who were born between September 1 and December 31, 1977; lived in the city of Oakland; and stayed at home during the day with either a parent or relative. Initially, public service announcements were sent to all local radio stations. We were invited to participate in a live talk show on a local, black-oriented radio station and gave various phone interviews with other radio stations. A write-up of the project appeared in the major local paper. Flyers were left in many community agencies, hospitals, and shopping centers. The publicity helped make TIES a viable project. Various members of the Oakland community came to the office or called to express their willingness to help and their support for such a project. Although we received many phone calls, most of the inquiries came from families with children too young or too old. After two months of heavy recruiting, we had only ten families (half of our projected goal) who fit all our criteria. Even though there were fewer children in our projected target population than we had anticipated, this worked out well in that it enabled us to refine our video and interview techniques. In this study we focused on toddlers predominantly being reared at home. Many black mothers who had children in our age group and were working and had full-time child care situations did not qualify for participation. We were also concerned that many mothers with infants at home were receiving AFDC, and we wanted to sample a broad range of socioeconomic categories. Thus, some families were not included.

Our goal to recruit a minimum of twenty families across the economic spectrum to participate in the project was met six months into the study. Fourteen of the families remained throughout the entire two and a half years of data collection. Others moved out of town or put their children in full-time day care or became unavailable due to personal family matters. Parents in the sample were relatively young. Mothers' ages ranged from twenty to thirty years and the fathers' ages ranged between twenty and forty, with one exception—one father was fifty-three years old. Over half were two parent families. The average number of children per family was small, only two. Eleven of our sample children were firstborns, and were "only" children when the study began. Subsequently, six mothers in our sample gave birth during the study. Income ranged from AFDC families to one father earning more than $30,000/year. Median splits show that the sample was well-balanced on important independent variables such as child's gender, birth order, family income, and maternal education.

The following data are responses to sixteen questions posed in the final interviews of the fourteen mothers who completed the full study. These questions focused on "race" and stress. They were part of over two hundred questions in each final interview, which lasted approximately three to four hours. Transcriptions of these interviews were as long as seventy pages. Our respondents were sad to see the project end, but wanted fully to provide their insights and have their voices heard on these important issues.

Results

This section of the interview began with asking respondents the following question: As a black parent, what are the most important things that you want to teach your child(ren)?

The mothers were very consistent in their answers. Self-esteem, self-respect, and how to get along in the broader society were the most common themes. Respondents were clearly worried about how their child(ren) would react to racism and many described a need to "buffer" their child(ren) from the possible mistreatment he or she might receive because of their race. The responses were as follows:

Case # 1

How important she is to herself. I want her to get around being black. I mean I want her to know that she's black, but I don't want her to put black in front of everything she does. I want her to take pride in herself as a person first of all, not make black, you know. I just feel like if she takes pride in herself, then whether she's black or yellow or white, it's not going to make a difference and she's going to compete with whomever, or whatever color. She's going to put herself right up there and her color isn't going to have anything to do with her success.

Case # 2

Love, understanding, and respect for other people and other people's feelings—I have to teach her that there are a lot of sick people out there and they could pick her out because they're sick. To have respect for herself and for others.

Case # 3

I'd like them to be proud of the fact that they are black. I think black is a beautiful color, it comes in so many different colors. I think it's really nice, it's my favorite color. I think it's very important for them to be proud of that fact and not wish that they were otherwise. I want them to grow up, though, with enough exposure of other different types of people, Indian, Mexican, other languages, etc. [I want them] to feel at ease with them so that they don't get it into their head that just because you speak Spanish, you're inferior—where he can be in a position where he can understand other cultures—you know, be they white, Mexican, or whatever, and accept them whether or not he wants to be a part of it. I would prefer that he wouldn't. [I would prefer that] he would feel strong enough about his culture that he wouldn't necessarily want to become a part of their culture.

Case # 4

I always tell Jennifer that by her being black, if she don't go to school then she's going to have a hard way to go. Because I always try to explain to her that the world is based upon white people and if she doesn't get an education she won't be able to back her own self up.

Case # 5

Feed them and make sure that they are comfortable and have nice surroundings or at least adequate surroundings and I give them everything they need and they get most of the things they want.

Case # 6

Self-respect and discipline.

Case # 7

How to get along with others. How to be responsible. That's mostly what I really deal with, you know—just getting along with other people in general.

Case # 8

Respect, ambition, and self-pride.

Case # 9

Respect for herself and others.

Case # 10

How to live in this world with other people. How to get along.

Case # 11

Respect in people. I want to teach them not to be close minded or narrow minded to the things that are going on. I want them to learn the mandatory things to be able to get over in the world.

Case # 12

The most important thing is right and wrong as a black parent and how to deal with society as it is and let him know that he's protected as long as he's at home, but when he gets out there in the world, he's not protected anymore. And teach him things that will prepare him to get out there in the street.

Case # 13

[To] know right from wrong and to be the best in what they do. Teach your child about the world out there.

Case # 14

[To] learn to be themselves, how to get along with people, to love and respect people.

It was evident that respondents wanted to prepare their children to get along in the world, even though they realized that the world may be an unwelcoming place for them. However, when asked about what type of coping strategies the respondents would share with their children, many of them could not really articulate specifics. One parent stated:

I think that black parents teach their kids how to cope; they've done it for so long it comes natural, coping and surviving. (Case #2)

When further probed about what these coping strategies were, this respondent discussed how parents teach by setting an example. A second parent actually provided an example of the type of coping skill she felt her son would have to develop:

[The] fact that they are black means that they are going to have to put up with a lot more. If your white boss calls you "Nigga," he's not going to get in as much trouble as if you turn around and call him a "white motherfucker" or "honkey" cause you're liable to get fired. Even if it's the other way around, he's the employee and you're the boss, it's liable to come down a lot heavier on you. You have to know what things you can "shine on" and what they should fight [for]. I mean there are some things that they are going to have to stand up and fight for because they are black and there are some things that they are just going to have to let shine on, just for their own survival. I mean if you fight every slur that comes out, you'll be fighting all of your life. I'd like [my children] to have enough pride, because if you have enough pride and self-confidence in yourself, you'll let a lot more things roll off your back than if you're insecure about yourself. (Case #3)

Other respondents also discussed the issue of needing to cope because they understood that their children might have people against them just because they are black. They wanted their children to be as independent as possible so that they would not have to deal with "the man" as often. Thus, getting a good education was considered a critical coping strategy. Mothers of girls wanted their daughters to be independent as well. One mother stated she wanted her daughter to know:

how to take care of herself. I mean physically and mentally you know I'm not knocking the black male and I'm not [knocking] the white male either, but now-a-days there are so many women that are by themselves, you know. Some women don't want to get married and some that have been married. I want them to know how to deal with being by themselves—knowing how to take care of themselves. I don't want them to depend on nobody else. (Case #7)

Another respondent, a mother of young boys, also felt that being educated and being able to assume responsibility was critical. She felt that young black boys have an even more difficult time:

I think it would be a lot harder for him to survive in this world than it would be if he were a daughter. I mean a daughter can always cop out and get married, "I don't want to deal, so I'll marry him and let him deal." I think it's just because of the way our society [is], nothing or no kind of slant on women. It's a lot easier for women to get out of a responsibility like that, than it would be for a man. I don't think it's any easier for a black woman, but I think that it's a lot harder for a man to cope. Most white women can make it whether or not they are married. They don't have to face the type of discrimination that black women do. You're a black woman and you say "I don't want to cope with those people out there, all they're going to do is put me down, I'll marry him and let him cope with it." I think black men can't cop out like that unless they want to become a pimp or something like that, and let the women take care of them or be a gigolo or something like that. Other than that, they are just going to have to face it, and I think my sons are going to have to have a little tougher skin or a little more tolerance to be able to make it. I don't want them to get to where they turn into oreos or anything. I want them to be proud of the fact that they are black and I do hope that they would have some kind of role when they grow up in showing people how a black person can be, you know [I want them] to make some kind of change in the type of stereotypes that a lot of whites have about blacks. I don't want them to be afraid of going into certain professions, because only white people are in them. I don't want that to stop them from doing anything. I don't want them to think that their color will ever stop them from getting what they want. I would like them to have enough confidence in themselves to go after it. (Case #3)

The sample children were approximately three and one-half at the time of this interview. Respondents were asked four questions about their children's awareness of racial identity.

1. Does (child) know the difference between the races?
2. Does (child) know that he/she is black?
3. Did you or your partner tell (child) about the difference between races?
4. Did you or your partner tell (child) that he/she is black?

The results are presented in table 4.1.

Table 4.1
Child's Perception of Being Black

	Yes		No		N/R	
QUESTION:	N	%	N	%	N	%
1. Knows difference	5	35	9	64	0	0
2. Knows is black	6	43	8	57	0	0
3. Tell difference	2	14	10	71	2	14
4. Tell is black	4	29	6	43	4	29

As indicated by these data, most of the mothers did not think that their young children knew about racial differences; yet, even fewer told their child about the differences. Those that did believe their child was aware gave these reasons for such beliefs:

She knows it's something because when she sees little white kids, she'll watch them. Maybe she looks at them and then maybe looks at herself. (Case #4)

Because one day about three months ago, we were looking at a book and I asked him something and he says, "Not that boy, right there, that white boy." I never set him down and said, "OK now see that's black and that's white and that's Chinese." I never said anything, but he knows. (Case #5)

Because we were out shopping one Saturday and it was this little white girl, looking at her and she says, "Mamma, this white girl is looking at me." I've never told Nikki the difference between white and black, not that I can remember. (Case #6)

Because he will pick up a magazine and say, "Mama, this is a white lady. This lady looks like Candy [a white relative by marriage]." I say, "You're right, it looks like Candy." And I don't really know where he learned white or black from, because I didn't really teach him skin color, but he just picked that up from someplace. (Case #8)

Yes, he knows the difference, he screams and hollers, he fears them [white people]. (Case #12)

Respondents felt their children were too young to discuss racial differences, although thirteen of the fourteen stated that they thought they would talk about racial differences with their children someday. The time and age most gave for this discussion revolved around the child's entry into school, four or five years old. Parents appeared to want to wait until the issue came up "naturally" or through an "incident" before launching into a discussion with their children regarding racial matters. Others just felt the issue was too complicated and wanted to avoid discussing it as long as possible. The following comments were made:

[I will discuss race after I see] my first sign that she has noticed skin color and makes an issue of it. When I was little, four or five, I was afraid to play with a black child that was darker than I was, I mean very dark. And I remember my mother telling me, "It can't rub off on you and you shouldn't be that way, she's a little girl just like you." That is the kind of incident I mean. (Case #1)

We think she's a little too young to understand, but we [will] tell her. Sometimes when I'm combing her hair I say, Kiki, you know black women have pretty naturals, pretty Afros. She needs to know there's a difference between black and white and that she can't do certain things that white kids can. She can do them but she won't get away with them and that they'll get a break faster than she will. I think I'll wait until something happens in school or something happens and she brings it up. That would be a perfect time to tell her. (Case #2)

When I found out I was black [in the 4th grade], I was totally shocked. I didn't think I was white, I just didn't know that there were any difference in people. And then when somebody called me a "Nigga," I was just crushed. I mean that was just really a blow to my heart. But I'm not going to just sit down and wait for it to fall on him. I'm going to make sure that he's proud. I mean I would love it if he never noticed any differences in people, but I do want him to be proud of his skin color and the person he is. Our family is just like a melting pot. Everybody ranges from dark skin to very fair skin. Even dark skin with straight hair to light skin with nappy hair or whatever way you want to mix it up, and it's kind of hard to explain to a kid about that. They don't really understand and this is about the clearest thing I could get to him, you know, "You're black, they are all black, be proud of it." I don't think he still understands it. It would be a lot less complicated if everybody was righteously black and it wasn't so much mixture. (Case #3)

I don't really know. I would probably just tell him that there is a difference, you're gonna feel different. If he comes to me with a problem about racism or about why this is like this, why his skin is darker then I'll just have to explain it to him, that everybody is different. Everyone is born different and that we're just one of the chosen people. Some of the people got chose to be black and there's nothing that we can do about it. [I will tell him] that he should love himself and respect himself and take care of his body and be the best he can in life because he's going to feel different. He's going to feel different than his white friends. (Case #8)

I'll tell her about the different colors of people. But I don't think I'm going to get off into the racism bit until she specifically has a question or a problem and then I'll sit down and tell her. (Case #9)

When he realizes it [the difference] then he'll come ask me questions about it. That's when it's going to come natural. OK he says to me, "Mama what is the difference about race and stuff like that?" I'll say, "Well Robert, we have white people, all of them are not like this—white people that dislike us because of our color. And then there's prejudice against a lot of the races period. Prejudice started with the white and it's passed through the blacks, and you know, each one of us have a kind of dislike for another race. That's not something I'm trying to teach you, but I'm trying to help you understand prejudice, in case someone will act on you because you're black. They will let you outright know that they don't like you because of your color." (Case #11)

Although most mothers stated that their children were too young to really understand racism, four mothers felt that their toddlers had already been discriminated against in public. Two respondents felt that their children had been treated differently than white children in stores; one felt this happened in a hospital; and the fourth felt a white parent did not want the children to play together due to race. The fourth respondent stated:

I said to myself, they were prejudiced. It is kind of sad because a child don't have hate in their heart, just the parents put that in their mind. It makes you feel funny.

We were interested in whether or not the respondents had to deal with name calling with children so young. We inquired as to whether their child(ren) had been called "nigger" since this word evokes such emotion. The vast majority of the respondents answered no. The two who responded that a white child had called their child "nigger" shared their experiences:

She said, "Momma did you hear what he said? [A white man used the word "nigger" in the restaurant the respondent was frequenting.] But I don't think he'll say it again—not in here." And I said, "OK". The guy grabbed his girlfriend and he walked right out. They didn't even order their food. I guess he felt silly cause she [the daughter] said it loud enough for everybody in the restaurant to hear it and they all turned and looked at him. And we could just tell he was turning red. My mother was sitting like this [embarrassed] and said, "Why didn't you talk with that girl?" I said, "Momma, I think she did right." She did right! There are other people in this world besides white. (Case #7)

[We were] in the store and she heard, "You don't want to play with that niggah." (Case #12)

Four parents also reported that young black children have called their children "nigger" in fun while outside playing with other black children.

Findings/Discrimination Dilemma

An interesting contradiction in the data appears when the discussion turned to the respondents perception of discrimination targeting themselves versus their children. We asked the question: Have you ever been discriminated against because of your being African American? Ten of the respondents stated yes. Below are a sample of responses:

When I left high school I went to the unemployment office for a job. There was a white girl there that was in the same class I was in. I was in front of her. All the jobs they showed me were maid and janitorial, you know, little jobs like that, baker and laundry. I started to talk to another girl and she went up and they told her they had a training position—they would train her for a certain position but they said they didn't have anything for me. (Case #2)

Oh yes, the first time I found out I was black. I brushed against this little white girl when I was in the 4th grade and she said, "Get out of my way nigger." I was looking around to see who she was talking to 'cause I thought whoever it was, was obviously the scum of the earth. 'cause I had never even heard that word before. And I turned around and everybody was looking at me, including her. I didn't know what to think. (Case #3)

One night we had gone to Fenton's Ice Creamery up here on Piedmont.   We had been there for about an hour before we were waited on. As we were sitting there getting ready to be waited on or whatever, I mean it was about two or three, maybe four, white couples who came in and sat down. And they were served so much earlier than we were until I couldn't really believe it, I was just looking. So I called the little white waitress over, she looked to be about twenty or twenty-one years old and I asked her, my mother was with me, "What are you trying to prove?" and she says, "What!" She was very nasty. And me, I don't know why, I'm not racist or anything but it makes me feel like, if I'm there before you I should be served before you, unless you have a res- ervation or whatever. If you don't, then it makes me feel that [the waitress] just has something against me because I'm black or whatever. I mean that's the first thing that pops up in every black person's mind to my knowledge. (Case #6)

There was an incident I remember very vividly. In fact it happened in second grade and that was the first real punch, you know, "I'm black." It had to do with the kids in the room. We were playing and talking. And we were supposedly have gone to the museum that particular afternoon. Two black kids in the room. Out of all the kids in the room, she picked the other black girl and myself to stay in the room while they went to the museum. And we had to write, I will not whatever, whatever in class. And so it dawned on me, "I'm black, so that must be it." That really stood out. (Case #9)

Four respondents stated that they had not been discriminated against. However, in the very next question, we asked the respondents to tell us if they had ever been discriminated against in a variety of settings. *All* of the respondents an- swered yes to three or more of the choices. This was even true for the respon- dents who had just told us that they had not experienced discrimination. One aspect of mundane extreme environmental stress is that it is often so taken for granted that people may even forget about it; it is such an expected or common occurrence that respondents may need prompters to identify the discrimination that caused the stress; the mundaneness of the racism directed toward the respon- dents illicits avoidance of identification. However, once the discriminatory act is identified, the respondents seem to remember with great detail what happened to them. Many get angry all over again. Their voices changed when they shared their experiences and a few even paused because the memory was so negative. One must keep in mind that M.E.E.S. is not merely the discrimination due to one's blackness, but it also embodies the specific type of interaction and reaction to this discrimination against blacks. Context must be incorporated. African Americans, due to our unique history in this country, are constrained not only by discrimination but also by the overwhelming consensus this history has created in the mind set of people: one that states "black is bad." At times parents, with very good intentions, try to avoid consciously thinking about it. It is painful.

It is limiting. It is acknowledging the powerlessness we often feel. It is stressful.

Table 4.2 details the type of places where respondents stated discriminatory acts had occurred in their life in order of frequency.   Nearly all of the respondents (86%) had had a discriminatory experience in a store. Typically, the respondents stated that they were in a store and were next to be waited upon. Instead of getting the service, the salesperson waited on a white person instead. Being ignored and not provided the customary service was a very common complaint in a variety of the locations. One respondent recalled when she was asked by her grandmother to go to the corner store to get a loaf of bread for dinner. Upon entering the store, the respondent got the loaf of bread and stated that the store owner saw her. There were two white people purchasing their goods. The store owner waited on them, but when it came time for the respondent to pay for her bread, the store owner said the store was closed. The respondent was extremely angry and stated that she "couldn't express my anger to this white man . . . and I couldn't go home and express this anger to my grandmother, cause she was of that generation." Another common feeling expressed by the respondents was stated explicitly by Case #8 when she said, "I really couldn't pinpoint it. But deep down in my heart, I felt like I was discriminated against because of my race." Case #4 voiced a frequently felt comment when she stated that discrimination is subtle these days because "they [whites] do it in such a sly way, you know, you really can't tell." Some of the respondents felt that they were paranoid about getting services since they were not sure if they received late, poor,

Table 4.2
Location of Discriminatory Acts

Location of Discrimination	Yes, Experienced Discrimination	
	N	%
Store by sales person	12	86
Restaurant	10	71
Job Seeking	10	71
Hospital/Clinic	9	64
School	8	57
On the Job	8	57
Housing	7	50
In a Bank	4	29
Social Serv. Agency	3	21
Recreation Facility	2	14
Public Serv. Agency	1	7
Bar/Disco	0	0
Other: Military Base	1	7

or inadequate services due to their being black or for some other unknown reason.   These are clear examples of mundane extreme environmental stress (M.E.E.S.). Such micro-aggressions happen so frequently some just ignore it, some may not be conscious of it, while others get highly angered and agitated.

When asked about their spouses' experiences, eight of the eleven respondents where this was applicable felt that their spouses had also been racially discriminated against. The other three stated they did not know because their spouses had not discussed it with them. The effects of this discrimination on the spouses was nearly unanimous—a strong dislike and distrust of white people in general and a sense of defeatism. This is expressed in the comments of the respondents regarding their spouses:

It kept him unemployed for a while because everyone where he went knew his manager [with whom the husband did not get along]. He felt awful, terrible, after four years and it was all down the drain. (Case #1)

I think that it really made him bitter; yet at the same time it gave him the will to strive and to really show them. (Case #5)

They made him feel inferior. (Case #8)

I know it makes him uptight. He doesn't really talk about it in depth. He might touch on something, then, I know that it really had to bug him in order for him to mention it. As far as his conduct, it doesn't change. (Case #9)

Yes, he has a very hard time dealing with white people period, in general. (Case #10)

[As a result] he just don't like them. (Case #11)

He won't fight. He'll just take it, whereas before, he use to be the one that would fight for it. Now they done got him to where they done did it to him so many times, he won't fight. He just says, well that's the way it is. But he don't like white people though [and] because of that he tells my kids to stay away from them. (Case #12)

When one considers that these men are fathers and are not the young African American men in the jail system, on drugs, or in trouble, one is saddened by the level of anger and amount of weight these men carry with them. The avoidance of conversation regarding discrimination with their spouses may be due to the perception that you can do very little to change things, so why burden your spouse with these incidents. It has an extreme impact on the psyche of the men and women who carry this burden, often alone. The previous example of the young woman discriminated against when she was getting a loaf of bread for her grandmother is a specific instance of carrying the burden alone. The woman felt she could not talk to the store owner or to her grandmother. This had to have placed added stress on her young mind. Coping with it alone may be seen as the only way, but it can exacerbate the individual's situation.   Often African Americans do not know how to take, or handle, these constant micro-aggressions on their minds.   Withdrawal, internalization, denial, transference, and projection may each be called upon as coping strategies.

The effect of M.E.E.S. on parenting is difficult to measure.   However, it is undeniably present as indicated by the vast majority of the responses provided by these mothers.   When asked directly about whether or not being black places an added stress on the lives of children and on the lives of parents, once again, we get mixed messages.   These data are presented in table 4.3.

Table 4.3
Added Stress of Being Black

Added stress on:	Children			Parents	
	N	%		N	%
Strongly Agree	3	22		6	43
Agree	5	36		4	29
Disagree	4	28		2	14
Strongly Disagree	2	14		2	14
TOTAL	14	100		14	100

Parents were ambivalent regarding the added stress placed on children as a result of their blackness. Slightly over half agreed that this stress is present:

Being black has caused a problem for years with black people. With our kids, we haven't advanced that much. So we still have a long way to go and we know that they're going to be subjected to discrimination and all the other things we've been subjected to except their discrimination is going to be done more intelligently it won't be as much in the open as it used to be. It hurts them in the long run. [How?] Not seeing a way out. They don't think they're ever going to get a decent job — making decent wages. And it just makes themselves put themselves down. It makes them turn to drugs and other criminal activities.   And then that way they [white people] keep us institutionalized. (Case #2)

A lot of black people have to prove more. I'm going to have to do better [than a white person]. If you were lighter it was equated with more beautiful and straighter hair was equated with more beautiful and more well mannered or they were able to get away with a lot. (Case #3)

It might make some feel they have an inferiority complex because they are black. (Case #6)

Being that they are so impressionable and they have to deal with the problem that somebody else has 'cause they can't get over them being black. Still they have to go to that person in order to get an education or whatever it is. So it is like you got your hand in the tiger's mouth. (Case #9)

Children are met with opposition that they don't even know about. (Case #10)

I guess because of being a black person you have to fight so many oppositions for your kids. And in a way you're living two different lives. You're telling them one way that they got to do this, in order to survive in this society, whereas you've tried yourself and it didn't work. And then you're placing that on your kids. I mean afflicting your stresses on your kids because things didn't work for you, but you still hoping that it will work for your kids when they get older but it don't. They still have the same problems. (Case #12)

Because the school that my little boy goes to now, he seems to think there's some type of prejudice that he pretty well understands. And one day he said, "The only reason why [the teacher] won't scold Brian is because he's white and every time we get into an argument, I'm always the one to be yelled at, cause I'm black." (Case #13)

Mothers were at times frustrated because they did not know exactly how to prepare their children to face racism, particularly these micro-aggressions. The fact that they know it exists and they hope for change, yet still must socialize their children to deal with it, poses a curious dilemma. I believe that one aspect of M.E.E.S. is denial and avoidance. In this study, there are many examples where the mother stated she had not faced discrimination, but when probed, she remembered many times that she had. In reference to those mothers who said their children did not experience added stress from being African American, their avoidance of accepting the possibility of this being true was evident in their comments and body language. One couple just stated that their children were too young and just did not know:

Well, kids really don't know what's happening and the adults do. (Case #14)

Others seemed uncomfortable and their responses indicated that the stress was in fact present, even though they had answered that they did not agree that added stress was placed on children, as in the following response:

I feel that it depends on how you bring up the child. Really, you could. It depends on how you bring up your child on how to handle it [racial stress]. (Case #7)

One parent just sadly stated that she did not know if her child felt the stress, but she probably would as she got older. On the other hand, there was greater agreement among the mothers that being black places added stress on the lives of black adults. Seventy-two percent (ten of the fourteen) of the mothers agreed this was true and had the following remarks:

You say, "Well Lord I wonder if my children are going to have to go through what I went through." Then you come home and like I've heard people come off their job and say, "Oh, that honky up there, trying to put me back." These are things that really make you feel like you're low. Makes you feel that your whole race is low. [It] just makes you feel like you're nothing. Then you say, "I wonder if my children will be treated the way I was treated". You just deal with it. They do it in a dirty, stinking, biting way where you're just hung between the ropes. It's nothing you can really do, 'cause you don't really know if they doing it or your mind is telling you they doing me like this. (Case #4)

We deal with it [black stress] with an innate sense of humor. It's pretty rare when you find a black person that doesn't have a sense of humor. Religion is a means of coping for some people. Family, and what I feel is that natural inner strength that black people have to just be funny. Let it roll right off their back and keep on stepping. (Case #5)

Well, the inner dislike builds a kind of fear of some white people. You feel inferior to them and you feel like they are going to do something to you. It is their way of making you feel inferior in some kind of way. We hide them [the fears]. I hide them. When I want a job, I'll just go and give them my best and just hide those deep-rooted feelings. (Case #8)

That's probably the reason why we're so messed up. Having to cope with stress, tension, or let's say you don't have a job—gotta go look for a job. Once you get out there you're going to have to cope with this mess. So you have to sort of psych yourself in a mind trip. We handle it by psyching ourselves out. Some of us say that we're dealing with it by verbally abusing each other, verbally and physically. Nowadays you hear of a lot of black suicide and you didn't use to hear that. It's the stress factor. (Case #9)

I think a lot of them [black adults] are trying to find ways to cope. They find ways using drugs or whatever and some of us deal with it by one day at a time and just taking it as it comes. And some just don't deal with it and this is why I feel we need help in mental health. Black people [believe] regarding mental health, "oh you are crazy people" [those that use mental health professionals and the mental health profession], and I don't want to be bothered with it. I think we should reevaluate mental health and realize that, yes, we could use some help. (Case #10)

This [the black stress] make them have a chip on their shoulders and be mad all of the time and hate white folk. It do. (Case #14)

These comments underscore the great impact of M.E.E.S. It is a combination of the day-to-day acknowledgment that the larger society is against you coupled with the constant fear and anticipation that something bad is about to happen to you just because you are of a darker hue. Even mothers who stated that there was not added stress in being black gave comments that seemed to indicate a dilemma:

Only if you let it. (Case #1)

I think it just depends on the person really. Because some people can deal with it and some people can't. With me, I ignore it most of the time. I just ignore it. (Case #7)

We're not going to get the best jobs but we can get a job out there making some kind of money. It may not be what your white counterparts are making but you know, if you work hard at it, maybe you'll get something decent enough to give your family some of the things they want. (Case #2)

The first response indicates that "it" exists and only adds stress to a person's life if that person allows "it" to. This response assumes a sense of control. It suggests that the adult "lets" the stress affect him or her or can "choose" not to let the stress affect him or her. The second response is similar. Once again it acknowledges the presence of "it," the stress of being black. The respondent puts the factor of control into the picture, "Some people have control and thus can deal with it and some can't." The third response is very perplexing. It assumes that getting a worse job or less money is not putting stress on the individual. Many would assume that this differential would definitely add to the stress of the job seeker. The notion of the Protestant ethic of working hard and getting just rewards is invoked in this response. However, the rewards are assumed *not* to be just, as the respondent points out that "we're not going to get the best jobs." A curious contradiction is implied in such responses.

CONCLUSIONS/DANGEROUS MYTHS

Being a good parent is difficult for anyone. I believe the data presented in this chapter provide valuable insights into the thoughts and feelings of a fairly typical group of African American mothers who are trying their best to raise healthy, happy children. I am postulating that their job is made more difficult because they cannot make the assumption that the larger society supports their efforts. Quite the contrary, they live with the knowledge and personal experiences that lead them to believe many people in this society, particularly those perceived to run the society, have strong prejudicial views against African Americans.

The mothers in this study consistently understood the need to teach their children to love and respect themselves. I believe this was so universal because they knew their children would need this self-love and self-respect in an environment where they would be constantly challenged to prove their worthiness. Phrases like "get around being black," "you can't wash it [blackness] off," and "gonna feel a difference [being black]" imply that being black can be a liability. These parents expressed their love for their children and desire and hope for them to be able to live in a world where their skin color is not considered a problem. However, they also see and experience the reality of racism and discrimination in their daily lives. Thus, as one parent stated, "It is like you got your hand in the tiger's mouth."

Children are not insulated from the stress their parents may feel as a result of daily coping with the tiger. The strategy of teaching self-love and self-respect is necessary, but not sufficient for helping children reduce their M.E.E.S. factor. Parents have to understand the psychological climate within which children must develop. Not being able to talk about racism because of parental embarrassment can be damaging to a growing child. Focusing too much on the inequities of the society may be equally damaging. African American parents must daily walk a tightrope of what to say and what not to say about racism; what to teach and what not to teach; what behaviors to model and what behaviors not to model; when to fight and when to accept prejudice; which ages are appropriate and which ages are not for such discussions. This all must be done while one is still dealing with the other daily physical and emotional needs of the family.

We live in a multicultural, high tech, too much information society. Each of us and the cultures we represent have much to offer. However, due to the media, certain school programs, some personal experiences, and other institutions, our children often do not see it this way. Too often our children are caught in a cultural conflict, whether it is ethnic or generational. Clearly, the primary social, psychological, and emotional needs of children are great and they certainly need guidance. Their developmental need and struggle for self-esteem, self-identity, independence, consistency, and order are compounded when their cultural ties are not stable and appear to be in conflict with the more accepted white cultural mandates. Black, white, red, brown, and yellow children are exposed to popular media, to conflicting messages, values, and perspectives. There are those who believe the problems of our young are merely a reflection of our own cultural schizophrenia, that we too often preach one thing and do another. We, as parents, must realize, accept, and act on the fact that we live in a very challenging time. When our children do not have a path to positive self-esteem, when their culture is devalued by parents and/or the larger society, when their skill levels are low and they do not see a means for their own success by traditional routes, they will create alternative routes as the sociologist Robert Merton (1957) suggested. The responses of our mothers indicate that they, too, understand this sociological phenomenon. Some of the children will redefine success; others may take illegal or dangerous routes; some will do fine; many will just drop out and not buy into the future, for to them, it holds no rewards.

African American parents, like many others, have bought into three dangerous myths that may unintentionally lead some of our children to take wrong turns in their quest for positive identity formation and self-esteem. The first myth is that all children are alike. Yes, children do have similar developmental needs and the same basic physiology. However, as black parents, we must realize that black children will indeed be treated by this society differently than white children. We cannot afford the luxury or "dream wish" of believing and telling our children: "You are the same as a white child and you can act the same." This is a dangerous message. It assumes that racism is dead even when our experiences tell us it is alive and unfortunately thriving. There will be times when our children cannot act the same as whites and expect they will receive the same treatment just as adults know that we cannot act the same as whites and get the same treatment all the time. All of the statistics regarding incarcerations tell us that if you are African American you will be stopped more often, arrested more often, charged with more serious crimes, and get longer sentences than your white counterpart (Carroll 1974; Debro 1977; Nelson 1992; Blumstein 1995). These problems of differential treatments do not start at puberty but are part of a continuing battle that starts when our children are mere infants. Over half of our respondents described the differential treatment received by their children in hospitals and clinics. Their children were infants at the time. Although our children are as bright, as talented, as gifted, and as beautiful, and are equal to any competition, if we fail to understand that they will be differentially viewed and treated, that they will experience the micro-aggressions and M.E.E.S., we are making a major mistake in preparing our children to cope. Many young people who have always thought they were "good," "bright," "worthy," and "self-assured" begin to question these attributes when they encounter differential treatment without any understanding as to why. There is a delicate balance that we, as parents, must begin to cultivate between teaching our children what they do have control over and what they do not, and even more important, how to tell the difference and how to cope with the consequence. I am reminded of the praying hands that my family gave me with the following inscription:

> God, grant me the serenity to accept the things I cannot change;
> the courage to change the things I can;
> and the wisdom to know the difference.

There is no precise prescription for the implementation of this strategy. Yet, parental awareness is critical for any movement to increase the ability of our children to handle M.E.E.S.

A second myth that can be detrimental is voiced by many parents of all races: "Since I went through that as a child and came out okay, so can my child." This statement assumes that each generation goes through the same types of issues and is equally equipped to handle them. This can be deadly for African American children. For each generation, the "ante" seems to have gotten higher for behaviors in which our young can get involved. For example, sexual promiscuity now can lead to death due to AIDS, versus the past fear of our parents' generation of pregnancy. There were many in my generation who experimented with marijuana with no long-lasting effects, whereas today's flirtations with drugs often mean crack addiction, a drug unavailable in "our time." When segregation was in force, many of our doctors, lawyers, and professionals lived close to the unemployed because they could not move to white neighborhoods. The "ghetto" had a somewhat different meaning then. The increased violence in our communities makes negotiating life in the 90s quite different from negotiations of the past. So, in fact, just because you went through childhood in a racist environment does not mean that your situations, strategies, and successes can be passed on without change or without contextual modifications.

The third myth is one that I feel is almost taken for granted in a capitalistic society. In our quest for economic parity and our desire to be treated as equal and get the best that money can buy, we often believe that if we have enough money we can pay for equality. This is very problematic for African Americans. The study parents described how they had money, went to the "best" places, and were still treated poorly. When it comes to providing services to our children, parents must be vigilant. A preschool that costs a fortune does not necessarily perpetuate the self-esteem building of a black child. The "best" schools money can buy sometimes still have very little in the way of multiculturalism. The "best" homes money can buy may be in environments where the child is forced to be the only African American in the "hood," and therefore the child may feel isolated or experience stress when he or she is thought to be different, or when he or she is not invited to a neighbor's party. Based on discussions with many middle-class parents, these experiences are common as the child approaches adolescence and dating age. In our desire to escape the many problems associated with class, we sometimes forget that there are also problems associated with race that transcend class. Believing that money can solve these long term and embedded racial issues is unrealistic and inconsistent with the data. For example, African American professionals with the same educational background as their white counterparts still, on the average, are paid less in every white collar profession for which data is available (Garwood 1992).

Believing in these myths is an attractive option for parents. We would all like to think that our children have equal chances because we are all alike; are equally prepared to parent due to our past experiences; and can buy into the American financial dream if we just work hard and buy the "best." However, belief in these ideals without placing them within the context of the contemporary environment within which our children live can be a fatal attraction.

Parenting is clearly not an easy task. I am sure every parent could easily recant horror stories about what this experience is like. I can recall my abhorrence of the baggy clothes, crazy haircuts, and blue/black lipstick of my adolescent children—not to mention beepers, late night calls, and young people who seemed to be speaking a strange form of English asking for my daughter by name. However, instead of sharing such stories, I would like to share some strategies that I have found helpful in meeting this parenting in the 90s challenge. It is clearly necessary for African American parents to engage in productive dialogue, to talk with one another, and to educate ourselves about ourselves and the dilemmas we encounter as black parents. Many of the study parents expressed their deepest gratitude to the TIES staff for allowing them to talk about parenting. The sample mothers felt by talking about, and our calling their attention to, parenting issues, they were able to be better parents. For some of us, family life is considered a private undertaking; public exchange about our joys and frustrations may seem a bit strange; even discussing racial problems is a taboo topic. We do not want to be considered too racially conscious. But as I described in the preceeding three chapters, many things are changing. There is no question that we, as concerned parents, must take stock of these changes. In some cases we must flow with them and in others we must take on the role of navigator and try to chart the course of future change for our children.

PARENTING STRATEGIES

The single fathers in chapter 2, teen mothers in chapter 3, and the TIES sample parents all have parenthood in common. They all want the best for their children. The following strategies are offered to help in this monumental parenting task.

- As concerned parents, we must quit merely assuming and assigning right or wrong, good or bad, when dealing with our children's behaviors. Instead, we must really try to understand our child's perspective; it is this understanding of why our children engage in certain behaviors that will help us provide viable and attainable options for them. The child, too, has to see the behavior as right or wrong.
- We have to quit thinking we can only give our children "our knowledge" and begin aiding them in developing the cognitive and social tools to assess our knowledge and gain their knowledge to live in their world. Their world is indeed different than the world in which we grew up.
- We must listen, which can translate into using what our children know to build on their capacity to learn more. If we feel uncomfortable about something that we should be discussing with our children, then we need to find a friend, a professional, a neighbor, anyone we can trust, whom the child can talk with about the issue.
- Professor Asa Hilliard once shared with me that we need to quit using what we think children know to estimate what they can know. There are two problematic factors with this mind set: we probably do not know what they know, and our estimations are probably way too low.
- We need to have high standards and expectations for our children, with an organized and structured plan to ensure that they can live up to these expectations. We should not tell a child he can be a doctor and then send him to a school that does not teach him the necessary skills to be one.
- We need to show/practice consistency in the values and messages we provide our young. The do as I say, not as I do, attitude has never been truly effective for any long term behavioral changes.

- Role modeling is critical. How can children be someone or behave in ways they never see? We must expose our children to a variety of positive models and positive methods of coping and thriving in an M.E.E.S. laden environment.

- Solutions must be contextualized and personalized. What works for some children or in some settings might prove disastrous in others. Children are individuals and should be respected as such.

- Children need to know that they are a valued part of our community, that they are valued and loved. We must do everything we can to build self-esteem, both personal and in regards to racial group identification. There is overlap between the two. It is perplexing and difficult to be a black child and think highly of himself/herself if we do not value black people.

- We need to celebrate the positive. Children need positive reinforcement and must know that their achievements are important. This should be a regular part of a parenting program.

- We need to seek out help if we need it. The thought that we can be supermom or superdad on a daily basis is asking for problems. Thus, surround yourself with a family support network of friends, family, peers, service providers, and so forth. Know where to go to get help before you are in a crisis situation. We not only need planned parenthood, but we also need to plan for parenthood once we are parents. We must start early!

Children grow older each day. They change. They look differently, speak differently, and think differently as they get older. Our early input helps shape these natural developmental changes. Finally, as parents we must give our children something to look forward to. In order for them to really become contributing adults, a desire to be a part of the future is mandatory. The "live just for today" attitude has to be tempered by the "I have a positive vested interest in being here tomorrow" attitude.

In a society where African American children are constantly exposed to the negatives regarding their blackness, it is crucial for the parent to emphasize the positive, to create some magic. Childhood is a magical time for our young, as it should be. Yet, this can be a trying time for parents who find themselves walking that delicate tightrope, trying to weave a sturdy safety net while simultaneously coping with child-rearing and M.E.E.S. This is indeed a challenge, a challenge we must have the faith and courage to meet each day for the sake of our children and our collective future.

5

A Challenge of Getting a "Good Education": Black Students on White Campuses

INTRODUCTION

The process of the selection of which college or university to attend varies tremendously from student to student. Countless variables play into the decision-making process: whether one's parents were alums, proximity to home, an emphasis on a particular major or field of study, how much scholarship is offered. As a high school senior, I knew that I was going to college, but I didn't have much information about the differences between college choices. The information available regarding ranking was addressed to the "generic" college-bound student. Ethnic/cultural issues were not mentioned except when demographics were presented or when special programs for "minority" groups were being described. My parents were not college graduates and just wanted me "to get a good education." I wanted more than anything to go away to college. I wanted to go away from home. I wanted to go away from the small town in which I went to high school. I wanted to go away from the military bases on which I grew up. I wanted to go away from my overprotective family. Simply stated, I wanted to go away. I knew that our family income would warrant a scholarship if I just kept making exceptional grades. I must confess, I also wanted to get a good education, but was unclear about just what that meant. Every brochure from every college I received stated that they offered a "good education."

The year I applied to college, there was a mini-push to recruit students of color. I say "mini" because in the late sixties the war in Viet Nam and the civil rights movement were in full swing. Malcolm X and Martin Luther King, Jr. had expressed their mutual concern regarding the consequences of the education and/or miseducation of African American children. Malcolm had been assassinated. Dogs attacking innocent protesters were being televised. Sit-ins, boycotts, freedom rides, and rallies were all part of the political landscape when I was in high school from 1964 through 1967. It was in this sociopolitical context that I had to make this major decision about which college I should attend.

I had applied to ten colleges and universities, based on the advice of one of my high school teachers. As I recall, my counselor was not that helpful in this decision-making process. She smiled a lot. She knew I was a good student. She was a nice, gray-haired lady who didn't seem to have a clue about the issues a young black woman would be facing in college, or in life for that matter. Like my parents, she stressed getting this elusive "good education." So she facilitated my getting applications, and I selected the colleges somewhat randomly—some in state, some out of state, some predominantly white institutions, some black, some large and public, some small and private, all, however, very prestigious by the descriptions in their brochures. I really don't know why I decided to apply to the places that I did. I *really* didn't have any idea as to where I wanted to go or the advantages or disadvantages of any given choice. Being class valedictorian, I knew I would get into some of these schools and so I just waited.

I got into all of the schools to which I applied. My family was very proud. My teachers were very proud, and I must say, so was I. But I still didn't know where I should go. I deferred the decision by saying that I would go where they offered me the most money. What I really meant was that I would go to the college where the amount of money that my family would have to pay would be the least. I chose Stanford—or maybe I should say Stanford chose me. With my big push to get away, I was a bit disappointed that Stanford was only one hundred miles away from home. But, I *would* be living away from home so my disappointment soon disappeared. It was quickly replaced by my anxiety about going to a place called "the farm" (I had no love for the country!), and to a campus where white people outnumbered blacks twelve to one! But they gave me a lot of money! At that time, the money was the most crucial variable—so to "the farm" I headed.

There were thirty-two African Americans in my freshman class. We were dispersed throughout the campus. Many of us felt that we were giving many white students their first multicultural experience. How do you get your hair to do that? Why does it do *that* when it gets wet!?! What is soul food anyway? I know you can't still be blaming me for slavery! Are blacks really more sexual? Can you teach me bid whist? Is there really such a thing as black English? Being a black woman trying to get a good education at this white campus was quite an experience. I did, indeed, get an education.

I find it a bit ironic that over a quarter of a century later, I am directing a program at the University of California at Berkeley dealing with the same issues I faced in 1967. Trying to find a way for African American students to realize their potential; to learn, grow, thrive, and graduate from a prestigious, predominately white educational institution. My official title is academic coordinator for African American student development. Black students demanded that this position be created in 1989. Their five-year graduation rate was less than 35 percent at that time, and many felt the problem was in the institution. Alienation, perceived hostility, lack of role models and support were all hypothesized as reasons for this dismal statistic. These perceptions held by students were also supported by the 1987 report of an academic task force, composed of faculty, staff, and students, on black student retention. One of the recommendations of that task force was the creation of a position specifically designed to support and facilitate the retention and graduation of African American students. No action was taken on this recommendation for two years. The students then went into action. A sit-in and a list of demands (very reminiscent of the 60s) led to discussions with the chancellor. My position was created and I began my responsibilities on July 1, 1989.

THE UNIVERSITY CONTEXT FOR M.E.E.S.

In my role of academic coordinator for African American student development, my primary functions center around facilitating retention and graduation of African American students. In order to do this effectively, I found that it was first important to learn about the context in which black students had to work, study, and succeed—which factors facilitated retention and graduation and which acted as barriers. Sounds simple enough, but in 1992, after three years, I felt that I was just getting a working handle on these issues. In my search for these answers, I was faced with three major structural barriers:

1. I learned that most programs do little in terms of evaluation, particularly, long term evaluation and process evaluation. For example, I was surprised to learn that until 1990, there was not any systematic evaluation and data on a very large summer program that specialized in providing services to Affirmative Action and Educational Opportunity Program students. I also learned that university withdrawal data was kept on a student *only* if the student came into an office and officially withdrew and completed withdrawal forms.

2. I learned that programs that state they are designed to serve underrepresented minorities systematically communicate and coordinate very little, if at all, with one another on the campus. This was not only true in general, but there was even less systematic coordination and communication in regard to a specific student's progress or lack thereof. This was particularly so across disciplines. It became even more evident in the time of fiscal cutbacks. Although supposedly serving the same populations, academic departments did not coordinate their class cutbacks with support service units that provided tutorials. It was as though the "academic" arena of the university was completely separated from the "student service" arena. Thus, writing classes in academic departments were cut simultaneously with cutbacks in writing tutorial and support sessions. This had very negative effects on many black students who felt they needed writing help.

3. I learned that even with sophisticated computers, keeping track of an African American student's progress was done in a cluster analysis format from year to year, so we did not really have good trajectory data on individuals. For example, the assumption was made that the four hundred freshpersons on whom you received data in 1989 would correspond to the sophomore data in 1990. Attrition,

transfers, new admits, students who did not get enough units to be considered sophomores, and so forth, were not accounted for in such data. Since each student had a student ID number, I made the assumption that trajectory data for any student would be easily accessible if I had that ID number. This proved to be a false assumption. Group data was kept by entry cohorts.

Overall, in my search for information and in my many discussions with faculty, staff, and students, I learned that African American students at U.C. Berkeley, like African Americans everywhere, share two commonalties. First, they are very diverse, clearly not monolithic. For example, regarding the single variable of financial background, freshpersons in 1992 came from families with incomes that averaged over $55,000 per year; yet one-third of them came from families with incomes of less than $30,000 per year. This is in an environment where white students had an average family income of well over $80,000 per year. Second, African American students do indeed experience stress just because they are African American, irrespective of their diversity, their majors, their high school records, their income levels, or their political orientations. The mundane stress of being black on white campuses has extreme effects on many of our black students. M.E.E.S. is clearly manifested and possibly heightened on predominately nonblack campuses. Variations of the following examples shared by my students are repeated regularly by black students who come into my office:

- I am the only black student in the classroom, a black issue comes up, and I feel all eyes on me. They expect me to be their expert on black people! Sometimes I have to remind them that I went to the same white school system they went to, and was not taught about our history or psychology or anything. Just because I am black they expect that I know all about the African American experience.
- I was walking down Telegraph Avenue on my way to class. I really wasn't paying much attention to the people on the sidewalk because I was in a hurry to get to class. But I did notice a woman grasped her purse more tightly when she saw me behind her. On another occasion, a white woman crossed the street! They both thought that because I was a black male, I was going to rob them.
- I don't like to raise my hand to give answers in class. I know that if I am wrong, the whole class will think that all black people are here due to "special action" and that we don't really belong here. My wrong answer will be used to justify their stereotypes. I don't want to take a chance and give them that satisfaction. I prefer to keep to myself.
- I was assigned this white roommate. She really thinks she's liberal and I almost feel that she uses me to make this point to others. Like she's saying, "See, I even have a black roommate."

Stanford psychologist Claude Steele (1992) labeled the experience described in the third example as a stigma, associated with racial devaluation. He described the double devaluation in such cases: risk devaluation from a particular failure (i.e., failed test or mispronunciation or wrong answer), plus a further risk that such performances will confirm the broader, racial inferiority that black students know they are suspected of having. Once again, this results in a unique set of circumstances for African American students—one that translates at U.C. Berkeley to high levels of repressed frustrations, to higher drop-out or "slow out" rates, and to lower grades. In other cases, this translates into students who feel they must overachieve to show the white folks that African Americans are smart and can excel even in this hostile environment. I agree with Dr. Steele that this devaluation, or in my view, another aspect of the M.E.E.S. factor, is one of the primary sources of under-achievement and attitude problems among African American students on campuses such as the University of California at Berkeley. It supersedes past achievement. True to the symbolic interactionist model, students must constantly respond to their perception of how others are viewing their presence. They are constantly reminded that they do not belong. They are constantly made aware that there is a common belief that black students are not as intellectually competent as white students. It is important to note that the student must cope with these issues whether he or she wants to or not because these false claims permeate every fiber of our society. The stress associated with being forced to even entertain these thoughts can interfere with one's academic pursuits.

One can fall into the trap of suggesting that African American students do not do well in such institutional contexts because they are not prepared or are less qualified. Some faculty and staff argue this point at U.C. Berkeley and even go so far as to say that Berkeley should simply underrepresent Chicanos and blacks and admit "more qualified" whites and then Berkeley would have a higher quality student body. Outside of some obvious flaws in this argument, a common false assumption that grade point averages and scholastic achievement test scores represent quality is made. However, if we look at the University of California at Berkeley students, past high school achievement does not directly translate into success. There is not the direct linear relationship between high high school grades and high U.C. Berkeley grades that is so often assumed. Most demographers and admissions officers will agree that we take the "cream of the crop" of African American high school students into schools such as Berkeley, many with GPAs exceeding 4.0 and with SAT scores in the top percentiles. Given these high levels of achievement of the vast majority of African American students who get into the prestigious white institutions of higher learning, how can one account for statistics such as the average GPA of the 1,596 African American students at U.C. Berkeley in 1992 being only 2.55? How does one account for over half of these students not completing their degrees in five years? These data are consistent with past research in which the overall progression rates of whites was found to be faster and their GPAs higher than their black counterparts (Nettles 1991). What can we do to resolve these discrepancies?

In order to gain insights into these questions, I met with staff at the University Office of Student Research to see what data were available on African

American students that could possibly lead to answers to such questions.   I learned that the surveys that were conducted with students had *extremely low* response rates from African American students, with the largest number of respondents being only forty. We then collaborated on developing a questionnaire. I was particularly interested in what stresses African American students faced in schools such as U.C. Berkeley. My task was to get a sample of African American students to complete the questionnaire—235 did. What follows are some of the results of this study.

AFRICAN AMERICAN STUDY SURVEY

Methodology

A questionnaire was developed that included questions previously used on a general U.C. Berkeley survey of students. Key questions focused on the use of campus support services, barriers to success at U.C. Berkeley, and future aspirations. Students were to respond to these questions by checking the appropriate boxes since most of the questions were forced choice or utilized three-or-four point scales. Demographic data such as gender, entry status, academic status, and age were also solicited. Finally, the questionnaire ended with three optional, open-ended questions: What was your best experience at U.C. Berkeley? What was your worst experience at U.C. Berkeley? Additional comments or suggestions? The questionnaire was marked "confidential" and students were assured that the data would be used for research purposes or for program development purposes only. It was three pages long. In addition to the questionnaire, many students gave verbal descriptions of their experiences on and around campus.

Our objective was to get a cross section of African American undergraduate students to complete the questionnaire, since the Office of Student Research had had an extreme paucity of black respondents answer any of their surveys. The respondents were not "randomly" selected by the traditional means. Our attempt was to get as many available African American students as possible to complete the questionnaire. Since the students were dispersed throughout the campus and many lived off campus, our task was a bit formidable. The surveys were distributed to counselors who work predominately with students of color, to the African American Studies Department, to African American student groups across campus and in my office. In addition, a table on the plaza where students pass between classes and during lunch was set up for questionnaire solicitation. During the 1991/92 academic school year, 235 questionnaires were completed for data analysis.

Findings/Sample Demographics

I first wanted to see how representative our sample was of the total African American student population. The Office of Student Research provided me with general demographic data for the 1,711 African American students for whom data were available at that time. Tables 5.1 and 5.2 compare our sample, representing 13.7 percent of these students, with the total black student population on gender and class status.

Table 5.1
Comparison by Gender

	Total Black Students		Students in Sample	
	N	%	N	%
Male	724	42.3	73	31.1
Female	987	57.7	161	68.5
No Response	0	0	1	.4
TOTAL	1711	100%	235	100%

Table 5.2
Comparison by Class

	Total Black Students		Students in Sample	
	N	%	N	%
Freshmen	265	19.3	43	25.3
Sophomores	300	21.8	32	18.9
Juniors	404	29.4	39	22.9
Seniors	406	29.5	56	32.9
TOTAL*	1375	100%	170	100%

*In the total students' sample there were 336 students without class information and in the study sample there were 65; these weren't included in the percentage calculations.

Table 5.3
G.P.A. Distribution

G.P.A. Range	N	%
1.0–1.99	2	1.2
2.0–2.99	91	52.6
3.0–3.99	79	45.6
4.0	1	.6
TOTAL*	173	100%

*Does not include the 62 respondents who did not complete this question

The study sample includes a higher percentage of women, freshmen, and seniors than exists in the total African American student population. The cumulative average GPA of the study sample is higher, at 2.92, than the 2.55 of the black student body. One must keep in mind, however, that the study sample GPAs are self-reports versus data from official records. Self-reports of GPAs are generally inflated. Table 5.3 shows the distribution of GPAs for the study sample. Even with self-reported data, over half of the sample have GPAs below 3.0, which is consistent with the national data.

The study sample is comparable and representative of the majors; the vast majority are in the College of Letters and Science (79% of the study sample versus 71% of the total students). The average number of units in which the study sample was enrolled was 14.4, which is also comparable to that of the general black student population. Seventy-eight percent of the study sample stated they have never been on academic probation. This is only slightly higher than the 75 percent of the total black student body.

Findings/Student Experiences

In an article entitled "Stress, Well-Being and Academic Achievement in College," Pillerman, Meyers, and Smedley (1991) delineated four important process variables impacting the academic success of African American students.   They are perceived supportiveness of the environment, degree of alienation, unique status-related pressures or problems (i.e., financial/personal problems), and the relative effect of using different adaptational strategies to cope with these pressures.   Students regularly relate stories of how unsupported they feel at the Univerisity of California at Berkeley. Many need "pep talks" to encourage them to continue. Each year I have over twenty inquiries about the Howard Exchange Program administered from my office because black students want to have the experience of feeling valued and in the majority, if only for a semester. In this survey we asked students to report their use of campus support services and indicate whether they felt the services were useful. The data are shown in table 5.4.

What really stands out in table 5.4 is that over 50 percent of the respondents have never used the services available. This is true for each of the listed services except for the college advisors and the major department advisors. Ironically, the highest percentage listed as "no help" is for the college advisors, followed by career planning and major department advisors. In two of these cases, students were required to use the services in order to declare majors or make any academic changes in their records. All of the other services are optional and require that the student seek out the service for use. On the other hand, the vast majority of the students who do take advantage of the services report that they are helpful. Are students not using these services because they feel alienated or not supported by them? Do students actually know that these services are available? Are they too involved with their other work (63% have jobs in addition to their class work) to make use of the services? There does not appear to be any one answer to these questions. All of them are true. Interviews with students indicate a wide range of reasons, and they vary depending on the perception of the service by the student. It is true that some students do not know of the availability of services. Inevitably, each semester black students who are in their junior and senior year come into my office requesting academic advising help.

Table 5.4
Use of Campus Support Services

Campus Service	Helpful		No Help		Never Used/ No Response	
	N	%	N	%	N	%
Student Learning Center Tutoring in:						
English	71	30.2	5	2.1	159	67.7
Reading	17	7.2	1	.4	217	92.4
Math	80	34.0	3	1.3	152	64.7
Science	38	16.1	1	.4	196	83.4
Social Science	34	14.5	2	.9	198	84.3
Foreign Language	12	5.1	6	2.6	217	92.3
Counseling Center	70	29.8	10	4.3	155	66.0
Student Life Advising (EOP/AA)	93	39.6	6	2.6	136	57.9
College Advisors	135	57.5	26	11.1	74	31.5
Major Dept. Advisors	122	51.9	15	6.4	98	41.7
Career Planning	82	34.9	18	7.7	135	57.5
Pre Grad/ Pre Professional Office	61	26.0	3	1.3	171	72.8
Athletic Study Center	29	12.4	0	0.0	206	87.7
Women's Resource Center	29	12.4	3	1.3	203	86.4
Re-Entry Center	14	6.0	0	0.0	221	94.0
Student Activities	58	24.6	1	.4	176	74.9
Disabled Students	14	6.0	0	0.0	221	94.0
African American Student Development	56	23.9	0	0.0	179	76.2

They have been at the university two or three years and did not know that the services of the Student Life Advising Center were available and had them as their specific target clients! Many confessed that they had thought that these services were only for students who were "special action" or had come in under special circumstances. In these discussions, I often got the impression that many black students wanted to prove they were not on the campus because of Affirmative Action, that they wanted to prove they could "make it on their own." Little did they realize that few, if any, students in these large bureaucratic institutions make it on their own. One student shared:

I know that each of these Asian and white students feel I am here taking one of the admission slots from a friend of theirs that did not get into U.C. I am a good student and I deserve to be here!

What defines being a "good" student varies tremendously from high school to a university setting. Many black students had to make a point of doing their work without their peers in high school since many of their peers were not doing well in school. Ogbu (1978) discussed this need of black students to feel they belong to their peer groups in high school. This is often at the expense of being perceived as a "good" student. However, doing one's work alone and not asking for help can have deleterious effects in a university where seeking out help is almost mandatory for success. The students who do not seek help may feel that reaching out would be admitting that they are not supposed to be on the campus—an admission of inadequacy. Since many of these students do not get very involved with their white or Asian counterparts, they have no way of seeing that these students do seek out help. Their perception of not being supported is then fueled by their lack of pursuing support services.

There are situations where students have sought support and felt that the staff person or program responsible for the support service was inadequate, insensitive, or just not worth the time. One student shared:

The program director just wants a "token" black presence. She really doesn't want to see me get ahead. I feel she is so paternalistic and she seems like she is doing me such a big favor by "helping" me.

Many students do not admit to having a problem, and perhaps some do not recognize that a problem exists, until they receive an unexpected low grade on an exam or paper. One of my Howard exchange students stated that having constant feedback helped her know where she stood. In many classes at U.C. Berkeley, one can go half the semester before a paper is returned or a midterm grade is reported. The assumption that the student was doing all right or well may be suddenly shattered. Then the task of what strategy to use to respond to the low grade becomes particularly stressful to students who may feel that the professor or teaching assistant do not care, or worse yet, do not think black students should be at U.C. Berkeley. Table 5.5 shows that over 68 percent of the respondents felt that getting to know professors was indeed a problem and 63 percent felt that dealing with race issues was a problem at U.C. Berkeley. Respondents seemed really concerned about making good grades even though over 45 percent of them indicated that their academic preparation for U.C. Berkeley was not a problem and over 44 percent indicated that dealing with a competitive environment was not a problem.

Seventy percent of the respondents in table 5.5 felt making good grades would be a problem, however, only 7.2 percent to 32.3 percent used any of the tutoring services offered (refer back to table 5.4).

It appears that many students may have had false expectations for the amount of work college required because over 60 percent felt that the amount of course work, balancing social and academic life, and the juggling of school and course employment were problems for them. Regarding the social life of students on campus, isolation, finding a boyfriend or girlfriend, and making good friends were not considered problems for over half of the sample. I asked about this apparent contradiction and was told by students that most of them live off campus, mainly neighboring Oakland, a city with a large population of African Americans, and don't feel that their social lives revolve around campus activities.

Table 5.5
Perceived Problems

Issues:	Serious Problem		Somewhat a Problem		Not a Problem		No Response	
	N	%	N	%	N	%	N	%
Making good grades	28	11.9	137	58.3	65	27.7	5	2.1
Getting into desired major	14	6.0	60	25.5	154	65.5	7	3.0
Deciding what to major in	25	10.6	79	33.6	127	54.0	4	1.7
Academic prep. for U.C.B.	31	13.2	93	39.6	106	45.1	5	2.1
My writing skills	17	7.2	96	40.9	117	49.8	5	2.1
My public speaking skills	20	8.5	85	36.2	126	53.6	4	1.7
Talking/getting to know professors on campus	63	26.8	97	41.3	72	30.6	3	1.3
Competitive environment	35	14.9	92	39.1	104	44.3	4	1.7
Juggling school and work	51	21.7	101	43.0	79	33.6	4	1.7
Too much course work	47	20.0	101	43.0	82	34.9	5	2.1
Deciding a future career	44	18.7	80	34.0	106	45.1	5	2.1
Dealing with race issues	57	24.3	91	38.7	84	35.7	3	1.3
Juggling school and family obligations	34	14.5	77	32.8	120	51.1	4	1.7
Distractions and family problems	41	17.4	88	37.4	100	42.6	6	2.6
Pressure from my family to do well in school	20	8.5	74	31.5	137	58.3	4	1.7
Making good friends	20	8.5	61	26.0	148	63.0	6	2.6
Feeling isolated	30	12.8	78	33.2	122	51.9	5	2.1
Personal safety in Berkeley	41	17.4	77	32.8	111	47.2	6	2.6
Personal safety on campus	39	16.6	78	33.2	112	47.7	6	2.6
Finding a boy/girlfriend	28	11.9	47	20.0	153	65.1	7	3.0
Concerns about date rape	20	8.5	57	24.3	152	64.7	6	2.6
Balancing social/academic life	34	14.5	114	48.5	81	34.5	6	2.6
Maintaining good physical health	35	14.9	74	31.5	121	51.5	5	2.1
Avoiding AIDS & STDs	11	4.7	26	11.1	191	81.3	7	3.0

Thus, their friendship networks extend beyond the campus community. This, too, can be a double-edged sword for academic achievement. While it is very positive that our students can find friendship and personal support off campus, this can take away from campus study time. In addition, the students' lives are not like those of the typical resident in Oakland or Berkeley. There is a different type of time demand, one that requires far more autonomous and constructive use of time.

Respondents were asked if they felt going to U.C. Berkeley was the best path for them to reach their goals. Seventy-two percent felt that it was the best path despite the difficulty many appeared to be experiencing. When then asked "What do you feel are some of the barriers to fulfilling your goals on the U.C. Berkeley campus?" financial issues were clearly the most pressing. Table 5.6 reports these findings.

Table 5.6
Perceived Barriers to Reaching Goals at U.C. Berkeley

CATEGORY*	Extreme Barrier		Barrier		Somewhat Barrier		No Barrier		No Response	
	N	%	N	%	N	%	N	%	N	%
Financial	70	29.8	60	25.5	45	19.1	47	20	13	5.5
Faculty support	25	10.6	71	30.2	58	24.7	66	38.1	15	6.4
Staff support	17	7.2	59	25.1	71	30.2	69	29.4	19	8.1
Advising	17	7.2	58	24.7	56	23.8	88	37.4	16	6.8
Housing	29	12.3	46	19.6	62	26.4	94	40	4	1.7
Personal/family matters	38	16.2	42	17.9	64	27.2	88	37.4	3	1.3
Academic preparation	23	9.8	45	19.1	73	31.1	75	31.9	19	8.1

*Students were also given the option of "Other." Two students stated stress, and one stated race.

Data from tables 5.5 and 5.6 are consistent regarding perceptions of academic preparation: approximately 30 percent feel that it is not a barrier and that making good grades is not a problem. However, nearly 10 percent feel that their academic preparation is an extreme barrier and making good grades is a serious problem. Over 40 percent believe that faculty support is a barrier versus 32 percent for staff support. The issue that seems to create the least barrier is housing. As stated previously, most black students do not live on campus. Nettles (1991) found that living on campus speeds one's progression toward graduation. Thus, although our students do not feel housing is a barrier, it may be working against their graduation time. Commuting, use of libraries, living with nonstudents, and other off-campus distractions, may be more problematic for off-campus students.

FUTURE DIRECTIONS

These data only begin to tap the myriad issues facing African American students on white campuses. There is clearly a curious mix of internal and external issues that interact to create success for some and failure for others. I have come to the conclusion that institutions of higher learning can do a lot to affect change in both the internal and external issues facing our students, and thus affect change in the too often negative statistics regarding retention and graduation of African American students. The perception of support is as critical as the vehicles for support. The students must be knowledgeable and feel comfortable using the support services offered on campus. This did not seem to be the case with the respondents. In order to match the perception of support with the actual services, I strongly believe that we must create an institutional understanding of the fact that it is okay to have an ethnic specific focus for some programs. Too often, one looks at multiculturalism and ethnic specific agendas as being mutually exclusive. Quite the contrary, they are both very much necessary for the success of large numbers of African American students. One cannot readily give in a multicultural setting if one does not know about, think positively about, and understand one's own ethnic specific self. One very powerful way of doing this is to make the university less large and intimidating by creating smaller "user friendly" communities within the community. At Berkeley there are a number of such user friendly communities that focus on ethnic specific issues as well as multicultural or majority issues. Such programs include:

- The Summer Bridge Program, where Affirmative Action and Educational Opportunities students, predominately African American and Latino/Chicano, come to campus for a six-week transition and acclimation program during the summer prior to their freshperson year. Data indicate that African American students who participate in this program get higher freshperson GPAs and have higher retention rates than black students who do not participate in summer bridge.

- Professor VèVè Clark in the Department of African American Studies, in collaboration with a variety of support services, has developed a course for incoming African American Students, AAS 39, Their University or Ours, Introduction to the University: An African American Perspective. In this class, black students have the opportunity to seek out the services of the university. For example, each student must work with a librarian and learn to do a literature review at the library, contact an assigned mentor, and take a walking tour of services on campus. In addition, critical thinking and writing are stressed as students read books about other students in similar white situations and learn how they negotiated their environments for success—one such book is Lorene Cary's *Black Ice*. Students who have completed this course also have higher retention rates and higher GPAs than students who did not.

- A faculty/staff to student mentoring program was established with the collaboration of the Black Faculty and Staff Organization (BSFO) and our office where each incoming African American freshperson is assigned to a black staff member in a very informal mentoring arrangement.

There are common threads in such programs that should be noted. In addition to being collaborative with a wide array of resources in the university, they each provide:

1. A supportive environment where the student is considered a valuable resource with much to give versus a liability or a deficient/disadvantaged student
2. A challenging environment where students are pushed to excel. Due to the acknowledged support of staff in these programs, a student is not fearful of constructive feedback
3. An environment that enhances risk-taking behavior versus depressing it—students are encouraged to speak out and in such environments feel excited about the challenge of the activities or of presenting an argument because they have come to feel comfortable in these settings. They realize that the staff knows they are intelligent and worthwhile, and they do not have to prove anything about being part of an "underrepresented ethnic minority"
4. A route by which a student has an identification with achievement
5. An avenue where black students are seen as individuals, not necessarily a token, representing the race
6. Staff who better understand the social/political issues associated with racism; staff who recognize that it is okay to be racially sensitive
7. An outlet to express concerns and feelings black students may have—the myth that "we don't even see color" in our society is debunked and the consequences of how we see color can be openly discussed
8. A directive pro-action versus reaction to the circumstances in which black students find themselves in traditionally white campuses
9. An avenue for African American networking
10. A follow-up with individual students
11. A forum for long term and short term planning—issues such as why am I here can be raised without condemnation or hostility
12. A psychological "safety net" for students who may feel there are few avenues for support in such a large, nonblack university

There needs to be careful planning of such programs so that the ramifications of all of the aforementioned issues are understood. Staff has to be sensitive to the issues of M.E.E.S. and how students must cope with it. Ironically, even though they are showing impressive results, such programs are being challenged and are targets for dismantling due to the anti-affirmative action proposition passed by California voters in 1996. Consequently, even more careful planning of such programs will be necessary.

African American students' reaction to the stress of their blackness and their perception of how others view and respond to them vary. Some take the "I don't need any help, I will show them that I can do this by myself" approach. As previously mentioned, this can be deadly in a university where no one does it by himself or herself. On the other hand, for a very few students, this motivates them to succeed despite the odds of doing so alone. Some channel their stress into anger at whites and the system. This, too, can lead to dysfunction in the predominately white setting. Others fall into deep depression and when they perform poorly, they start living out a self-fulfilling prophecy of failure. Many meet the challenge by seeking the necessary support for success. Some use the M.E.E.S. factor to fuel their energy and become super-achievers. Too often, however, the lack of understanding of M.E.E.S. and how our students negotiate it, leads to programs that further stigmatize our students in a negative fashion. The deficit model that assumes that there is something wrong with the student and if we fix it, the student will succeed is extremely problematic and deleterious to our future. It clearly sends the wrong message. Institutions can and must change this message and develop well-planned and informed internal programs of support if our communities are to be served by our students really getting and reaping the benefits of "good education."

6

Professional Sisterhood:
Standing in Stellar Space

INTRODUCTION

Each year at the University of California at Berkeley, a young group of incoming freshpersons participate in the Summer Bridge Program, described previously in chapter 5. Each year, as part of a professional role-modeling component of this program, I am asked to present a short talk on how I chose my profession. I always feel a bit guilty when I enter the room and see the eager eyes looking with the anticipation that I will be able to show them a clear path to professional success. I would like to go in and say that I knew that I wanted to get a Ph.D. and teach and do research ever since I was in high school or college. I want to present a picture of a focused professional with the right answers, and the tried-and-true tips for success. But honesty prevents me from appearing so organized, so together, and so directed toward my pursuit of the Ph.D. My story is much more meandering, a lot less linear.

When I was in high school, I didn't know what a Ph.D. was. I don't even recall meeting anyone with this degree and, certainly, I didn't know any African American woman with it. At my high school graduation, when asked what I wanted to be, I didn't have a professional answer as did many of my peers who said doctor or engineer. I always answered, "I want to be happy." As a freshperson in college, my goal was to get through the first year requirements and then worry about what I wanted to be. I really didn't know. Finally, toward the end of my sophomore year, I had to choose a major. I *still* didn't know what I wanted to be. I knew I didn't like anything that would require working with blood or illness, so I couldn't be a doctor (I get nauseous when others get nauseous). I was terrible with handling my own money, much less someone else's, so business was out. I had a problem with the use of the words "cunning" and "conniving" as positive descriptors, so being a lawyer was not even a question. My facility for drawing was called into question by the second grade students I tutored, so the engineering and architecture fields were not options either. (I used to hate it when I saw how *neat* the notes of engineering students were.) So, to help me with my dilemma, I went to the Office of Records and got a copy of my transcript. Looking over it carefully, I learned that I had taken quite a few sociology classes and that I had received good grades in them—so I majored in sociology. I loved working with the students in the community. So I decided I would be a teacher.

Because of my involvement with a couple of tutoring and reading programs, and my love for children, I applied to the Stanford Teachers Education Program (STEP). It was a quick master's and teaching credential program of four quarters, and I thought it would provide me with the necessary skills to do my teaching thing. Boy, was I idealistic and wrong. I was placed as an intern teacher at a high school in a neighboring district. I was to teach black history. This was in 1971, and this internship was an attempt to help this high school diversify its staff. There were only thirty-five black students at this school of hundreds, but I thought it would be a great opportunity to give these students a relevant class and a role model. I think the only other black teachers were in physical education. The staff of the school was not so idealistic. My few black students came in regularly with problems they were having—such as getting kicked out of school for wearing a hat, talking back to teachers when they didn't agree with what was being said in a class, and a variety of other "bad attitude" issues. I found myself defending and trouble-shooting for them more than teaching black history. My class was brought up at the board meeting of the district for being "racist" because I allowed the Black Student Union to use the classroom space after school for meetings. My Stanford advisor came to my defense regularly, but he admitted that he had no idea how to reach and teach the students who I felt were most vulnerable at this school. I would have to fend for myself and learn by trial and error. I did.

I admit, it was not what I expected. But it did put me on the Ph.D. path. One afternoon a student came and asked me to sit in on a discipline hearing he was having with one of the administrators. He was fearful that the administrator would not be fair and not listen to his side of the story. I agreed. When I entered the room for the hearing, the administrator, an elderly white woman, frowned at me and asked what I was doing in the room. I told her I was invited by my student to sit in. She became enraged, turned red, and said that she had a master's degree and knew what she was doing, that she didn't need an intern looking over her shoulder. (I really knew she meant that she didn't need a "nigger" looking over her shoulder; I could tell by the inflection in her voice.) It dawned on me that this woman really thought the degree mattered, that it gave her some special power to know what to do and how to do it. I knew beyond a shadow of a doubt that this was a very false premise. However, something clicked in my mind at that very moment. I decided at that point that I would get the highest degree in my field so that when I had to deal with such irrationality, when my motives for helping black students were called into question in the future, I could chime in with "and I have my Ph.D.!"

Three and a half years later, in 1975, I got it. I got the Ph.D. because I was able to find a peer group to support me in my efforts. I got it because I had a family backing me 100 percent. (After all, I was still considered the perfect daughter!) I got it because I was motivated by the many young African Americans who shared one common complaint: "They look at me but they don't see me; they hear me, but they don't listen." Our perspectives, our reality, our mere existence are often not recognized nor understood in classrooms across the country, be they elementary or university classrooms. The fatigue of the constant battle of making sure our voice is heard is a very common issue for African American professionals. In many university settings, particularly institutions with a majority of white students, black professors constantly complain that they are not given credit for the additional work they must do because of the need for black students to have a voice. Often our students will seek out black professors to discuss issues or racism, to ask for advice, to provide mentorship, to find a psychological safe place to rest. Many black professors take on the role of advisor/mentor to all black students, in addition to their expected university roles. They feel the mundane extreme environmental stress of being the black face in the sea of white faces on such university campuses. Many empathize with the struggle of the black students and know that they may be the only ears that listen or eyes that see them accurately. Many black academicians know the topics of their research interest may be put down by their white peers as being insignificant; their scholarship may be called into question just because they are black; their presence on committees may represent the singular black voice. The quest for promotions is often left in the subjective hands of the "old boy network" of white colleagues, mainly white men.

To an African American woman, such as myself, these issues are even more pronounced. The ratio of African American women to African American men in institutions of higher learning has steadily increased over the years. Data from the *Black Americans: A Statistical Sourcebook* (Garwood 1992) show that 9.8 percent of the total student enrollment was black in 1975, with men representing 5.6 percent and women 4.2 percent of this figure. In 1989, the numbers increased overall and shifted by gender. The total enrollment percentage of blacks was 10.2, with men representing only 3.9 percent and women 6.4 percent. Black female students were now in such institutions in higher numbers than their black male counterparts. Their need for role models, mentors, and advocates in their battles against racism and sexism seems imperative for success. In addition to the rigors of academics, the stress of not having good ratios of black men to black women on their campus probably added even more stress because black women have been hesitant to "cross over" in their dating patterns. I believe this to be yet another factor in M.E.E.S.—the day-to-day knowledge that there are not a lot of black men in your academic circle, that many of our men are being pushed out, left out, and burned out prior to even getting to college.

Working with African American college students, both at the undergraduate and graduate levels, I was curious to learn how M.E.E.S. manifested itself for women in other professions. I wanted to learn how other black women who have reached the top of their academic ladders by getting the highest degrees in their fields felt about the stress of being black, particularly in the context of also being professional and female. This curiosity led me to survey and facilitate two focus groups of African American female attorneys and doctors. The data presented in this chapter emanate from the participating African American professionals, these sisters who are indeed standing on stellar credentials. They realized that being a woman in our society has been devaluated and there are particular stresses and even greater devaluations in being a black woman. Most of them have used the M.E.E.S. factor to propel themselves forward. They have transformed the M.E.E.S. factor into a motivation factor; a challenge they were determined to win.

IN FOCUS: BLACK PROFESSIONAL WOMEN

Methodology/Sample

In the fall of 1992, two focus groups were held in Los Angeles, California. Recruitment consisted of contacting members of the Black Women Physicians and the Black Women Lawyers professional organizations. I shared with them my desire to conduct these focus groups. I gave them a set of criteria for participation: African American female; thirty-five and over; single; no children; willingness to share experiences in a group setting. I specified over thirty-five because I wanted focus group members to have been in their professional arena for a while. Since I was only conducting one group per profession, I also wanted to narrow the variables and have participants feel they had a lot in common with one another. Hence, I did not want to mix married and unmarried participants, or participants with and without children. I based this group makeup on the assumption that there are different factors that affect one's life with the added responsibility of a spouse and children. I also wanted to have the participants discuss issues about the availability and support of African American men from the perspective of single women. This was conceived as a pilot for future research in the area of professional black women, and I would love to facilitate future groups with married black women. These decisions were made not to exclude any perspectives, but merely as a beginning. Each participant also completed a brief written questionnaire.

The black lawyers' sample consisted of seven participants whose ages ranged from thirty-five to forty-three. Their mean age was thirty-eight. The black physicians' participants consisted of five participants whose ages ranged from thirty-six to forty-two, with a mean age of thirty-nine. Most of the participants were not born in California (none of the physicians and only two of the lawyers). One of the physicians, however, moved to California as a very young child, and two of the lawyers have spent almost all of their lives in California. The average time spent in California was between twelve and thirteen years for each of the two groups. None of the physicians completed their undergraduate degree in California; they attended such schools as Spelman and Bryn Mawr. Regarding their medical degrees, these, too, were completed mostly out of state (four of the five went to Case Western, University of Florida, University of Alabama, or University of North Carolina at Chapel Hill). On the other hand, four of the seven attorneys did their undergraduate work in California (at Stanford, U.C.L.A., and two at U.S.C.), and five listed California law schools for their J.D. Harvard, Bahara, LaVern, and Columbia were the out of state schools attended by the attorneys. Only one of our participants did not go to graduate school immediately after completion of her undergraduate degree. Since graduation from medical school, our physicians have had an average of 2.8 professional positions with a range of one to six different jobs. Their mean income was $163,000 per year with a range of $120,000 to $300,000. The attorneys had an average of 3.4 professional positions with a range of two to six jobs. Their mean income was $112,400 per year with a range of $55,000 to $160,000. When asked to describe their job satisfaction on a five-point scale, with extreme satisfaction on one end and no satisfaction on the other, all of the respondents answered extreme or a lot of satisfaction, as described in table 6.1.

Table 6.1
Job Satisfaction

	Doctors		Attorneys		Combined	
Job Satisfaction	N	%	N	%	N	%
Extreme	4	80	4	57	8	67
A Lot	1	20	3	43	4	33
Some	0	0	0	0	0	0
A Little	0	0	0	0	0	0
None	0	0	0	0	0	0

When asked about their family in terms of warmth and affiliation, most of the respondents stated that their families were very close or close. Table 6.2 presents these data.

Table 6.2
Closeness of Family of Orientation

	Doctors		Attorneys		Combined	
	N	%	N	%	N	%
Very Close	0	0	1	14	1	8
Close	4	80	2	29	6	50
Average	0	0	3	43	3	25
Distant	1	20	0	0	1	8
Very Distant	0	0	0	0	0	0
No Response	0	0	1	14	1	8

Family Background

Focus group participants came from a wide variety of family backgrounds. Most grew up in mid-size families with the average number of children in the doctors' family of orientation being four, and the lawyers' being three. Family size was upwardly skewed, however, as within each group of women, one participant had a large family; one lawyer had fourteen children in her family and one doctor had ten. Thus, the modal family size of one or two children was closer to the typical family size in both groups. One doctor had parents who were also doctors and two attorneys had an attorney for a parent. The rest of the sample came from predominately working-class families, both blue collar and white collar. Family occupations ranged from farmer and sky cap to medical technician and teacher. In their self-reports of their family's income and living environment while growing up, six of the participants described theirs as lower/middle class, three stated middle class, two stated lower/poor, and one stated upper-middle. Of the twelve participants, eleven provided birth order data. Six of the respondents were the firstborn in their families, three were second, one was eighth, and one was ninth. Four of our participants had a parent who was deceased—three fathers and one mother. Five participants had parents who were divorced; four had parents still together; and one had a mother who was never married.

It has been reported that there is a gender difference in regard to how children respond to authoritarian and strict parenting (Heiss 1975; Hill 1972; and Peters 1976). Black women are reported to fare better under these circumstances than black men (Baumrind 1972). In reference to this, our sample women were asked to describe their parents' parenting style on a scale of very strict to very lenient. Eight of our respondents stated that their mother was either very strict or strict, two reported average, and two lenient. Of the nine respondents who answered this question regarding their fathers, four stated strict or very strict, four average, and one lenient. Three in our sample did not respond to this question. Strict is clearly a more common style within this sample than is lenient. Most of the respondents also described their achievements as higher than that of their siblings. Five of the seven attorneys reported this as did three of the five doctors.

Facilitators and Barriers to Professional Choice: M.E.E.S. in Motion

It was surprising to hear how important the television was in our respondents' decisions to become attorneys or doctors. Dr. Kildare, Ben Casey, and Perry Mason had a major impact on a third of our sample:

I loved Dr. Kildare and Ben Casey. Television inspired me. Then my mother became ill. It was very stressful for me. I asked my mother what was wrong, and she said the doctors didn't know. I said if I had been your doctor I would have known. I wanted to be a doctor because I wanted to be able to tell people what was wrong with them.

Television influenced me. Dr. Kildare and Ben Casey. By the time I was eight or nine I knew I was going to be a doctor, a pediatrician. I never departed from that.

Perry Mason was the man. I wanted to be like him.

Attorneys cited that issues, such as getting to know the system so that it could work for African Americans, and feelings of empowerment, influenced their choice to become lawyers. Both doctors and lawyers emphasized that the desire to help others influenced their occupational choice. However, the choice was often difficult, given both their gender and their ethnicity. Many participants shared stories of how parents as well as teachers and counselors in high school and college did not think their choice was wise:

My father told me when I was around sixteen that I needed to be more reasonable. Then I decided to be a medical technologist. That was reasonable. I had never seen a black physician. There were no role models. My mother's doctor, a black man, took me under his wing. Nobody in my family believed it was possible for me to become a doctor. My mom didn't want to go to medical school because she was afraid she would fail.

At about ten, I decided to be a doctor. I've always been on that track. My mother told me, "Look, you need to go to secretarial school, get yourself a good job that you can rely on." Our parents didn't want our feelings to be hurt. We had to be realistic. Even when I graduated with two degrees, chemistry from Spelman and chemical engineering from Georgia Tech, mother told me to settle down and become an engineer, not a doctor.

I was in the top 5 percent in high school and president of the honor society, but in college I got slapped in the face. I went there feeling good about myself, but now I was competing with other presidents of honor societies. I learned very quickly that I didn't know how to study. My first two years were traumatic. After my first, I had an advisor tell me I was not going to medical school.

I was discouraged from going to college by high school counselors. I was the only African American there. In high school, my principal encouraged me to be a lawyer. My counselor pushed me toward technical school. She told other white students to go on to college, though. This angered me. This girl wasn't one of the brighter students either.

I was told when in college, "Don't study too hard, not good for your personal life."

I took German for a day. The professor called other students Mr. and Ms. so and so but called me by my first name. I wouldn't answer. I realized he was in a position that could screw it all up for me. We argued back and forth about the name issue and I finally dropped the class to avoid him. I didn't try to fight it because I didn't know who my allies were. I had no reason to trust the others in the department. I didn't want to be a troublemaker.

Many of the participants were sufficiently angered by those who did not feel they could do it and became even more determined to be physicians and lawyers. The support of family members, for some, was the major reason for their choice and success. The fact that there were few role models for our participants was a double-edged sword. On one level, they had no one to look to for guidance and to help them understand what they would have to endure in following through with their decisions to become doctors and lawyers. Yet, this lack of models made some feel a great need to be mentors and models for those coming behind them. They were breaking new ground. A consistent theme of the respondents was the support of friends and family. In two cases, the support of a black environment helped them mitigate the effects of a nonsupportive white college situation:

[What kept me going] was the encouragement I received early on from family and friends. If those people know I could do it, then who was this counselor to tell me I couldn't. I stepped back and realized those people couldn't be wrong. Also, I thought if I couldn't be a doctor then what else could I do? So I got a job as a nurses aide. I loved it, and it gave me the exposure to the medical field I needed. After seeing various roles, I reassured myself that being a doctor was for me. Other people around me were always supportive.

I went to an all black high school where 75 percent of all graduates went to college. I don't know what percent finishes. If you wanted to go to school, the school staff would get you loans, etc. We were almost assured spots at Norfolk State. If you wanted to go to school, you could go. My high school environment gave me the "you can do it" notion. In college, which was predominately white, I told myself that I wouldn't be at the top of the class. During class, I was shocked at how poorly behaved the white students were. The first exam, I realized that I could do it and I was a better student than the white students.

I had two role models. Both my parents were doctors. I chose medicine in junior high. I chose this because it was the path of least resistance.

As a senior in high school, I decided on medicine through a recommendation from my brother-in-law. There were no black physicians around when I was growing up no role models. But my parents never discouraged me.

I went to Spelman and the environment was very conducive. Because I was in a dual degree program, I got insight that many didn't have. I got the home environment of Spelman. I was expected to score well on exams, shooting for a 4.0. At Georgia Tech, I saw the frustration of black underclassmen. As an upper division student, I was mystified by how unhappy people were. Although they had the libraries, computers, etc., at Georgia Tech, at Spelman I got the nurturing. I belonged there. It got me through.

Participants were all in agreement that the course of choosing a profession and then following through with the training were challenges. Some believe they were just naive and did it because they did not know any better, or because it just never entered their mind to not have high goals and aspirations, as indicated in the response below:

It never occurred to me that I couldn't be a doctor because I'm a woman or my race.

Overall, however, as previously indicated in table 6.1, these professional women were satisfied with their work, even though ten of the twelve respondents listed work-related issues as their greatest stressor (see table 6.3). Clearly one of the hazards of being a professional African American woman is how one is viewed in the workplace. It is not surprising that so many of our respondents list work as a stressful environment. They articulated these concerns well—concerns that so readily can be defined as mundane extreme environmental stress; concerns that have to do with the day in, day out stressors with which our respondents are forced to cope if they are to maintain their professional status; concerns that make them feel as though they are being "watched" more closely, that their mistakes will be taken more seriously, that they indeed are getting a negative differential treatment just because they are African American:

If a black person offers a solution to a problem, it's overlooked until a white professional suggests the same and then it's taken seriously. This happens all the time.

They don't see who I really am in a professional setting. In order to be successful, you have to play a certain role. [You] always have to overcompensate. We don't know when we can let up. I assume that all people stereotype me into a certain role, therefore I overplay my role.

A white lawyer saw a client and had on different colored shoes. When the client asked about it, the bosses said, "Do you want a good lawyer or someone dressed for G.Q. " The white man can get away with that. Black people say, "I want my lawyer to look like something."

I feel that I can't make mistakes. I'm not sure I'm watched more closely, but I can't make mistakes. I practice in a predominately white area. At first, at meetings, I didn't realize that I was the only black there. I felt like I was doing most of the talking. Then I realized that I also was the only black and the only woman!

Sometimes I felt like they were ignoring my presence. They didn't believe I was a doctor. They [the nurse, and so forth] thought I was something else and were rude. Even if I weren't a doctor, they shouldn't have been rude.

There is this notion of "I can't be wrong." There is a pressure to always be right because if you mess up, everyone knows you did it.   During our residency at UCLA, black staff were very protective of us, very supportive. To mess up, it looked not only bad on you, but everyone.

We set the trail, if we messed up, they, the admissions office, etc., would not let many of us in.

I am automatically defensive. I believe people think that I'm not as intelligent, motivated, etc. [as my white counterparts]. I come in playing and overplaying that role. If not, people will walk all over you, whereas, white women don't have to do that.

There have been times when I 've pointed out mistakes of my white colleagues and I have been ostracized, while they aren't reprimanded. Had the shoe been on the other foot, I would have been fired. This is an additional pressure. You know you won't be treated the same way.

Table 6.3
Greatest Stressors

Respondent # L = Lawyer D = Doctor	Response
1L	Workload; lack of support; having to be responsible for family
2L	Racism, sexism by men and women and family financial stress
3L	Office politics, needing to prove myself repeatedly
4L	Work and sometimes dealing with family
5L	Job
6L	My job; personal life—not being married and having children
7L	Requirements of my job and dealing with opposing counsel
1D	My ex-husband
2D	Physical fatigue from long hours causes very low tolerance for other stresses
3D	Time management
4D	No response
5D	Work decisions

There is the pressure of always being right, because if you are wrong everyone will know, because you are one of the few, if not the only, African American. You stand out, even if you do not want to. This is not only a factor when dealing with whites. Our participants also indicated that there is stress placed upon them by other African Americans who may not have anything to do with their profession. Parking attendants, nurses, mail clerks in their offices, maids, and a variety of other service employees take a special interest in "the" black attorney or physician in the firm or hospital. Because there are so few black women at this level, the support staffs take a great deal of pride in the accomplishments of these professional women. Although this is meant to be complimentary, it can create added stress to be perfect, to look perfect, and to always be happy and up-beat:

I'm in a firm with 200 people. I feel like when I walk in the room, I am being scruti-nized. When I walk into the mailroom, they [black mail clerks] say, "Hello, Ms. [name], I really like you, you are down to earth. And you look very lovely today." Would he tell Mr. [white male attorney] that he looks very handsome today? Every-one has something to say about how I look—it is an added stressor, but it's not one to pay attention to. Just build that one in—you can't waste time thinking about it. I know I have to keep myself up because I know when I go in a room full of white men, they can't believe I am the [title] lawyer. You damn near have to close mouths. So I don't even think that I can get away with not doing my hair, etc. [they would have something to say and hold it against me].

Thus, this respondent realizes that the mail clerk is not trying to be demeaning, but at the same time, it is clear that different treatment is given and that added pressure is present since this lawyer cannot just be inconspicuous. This is cou-pled with the fact that once the black attorney or black doctor leave the service employees, she must then deal with her white peers who also think she repre-sents the whole black race:

Then there is the issue of speaking for all black people. You *are* the black opinion. During the riots, because many of the nurses I work with are Korean, I heard them whispering like I represented all black people. Unfortunately, in those situations, you do represent the *whole race*.

In addition to the pressure to be better, look better, and do better because all eyes are on you, the respondents shared how their roles are daily misjudged by others. One respondent shared an incident where the nurse would not give her the chart because she thought that the black physician was an orderly or another nonim-portant person. She had no idea that this African American woman was the at-tending physician. A couple of attorneys shared how shocked other members in meetings were when they walked in as the attorney in charge. Differential treat-ment by colleagues is a common complaint, as is the need to be more "official" or more "in control" in these settings so that you are afforded the proper respect. This poses a dilemma for African American women. As one respondent put it:

it causes women to be very schizophrenic. Professional black women are seen as strong and [as] people who take control. Then black women are less ladylike or less valued than white or other women.

Most respondents believe this issue of being ladylike versus being strong is a real barrier for them in relationships (Wallace 1979). Some do feel that they have to be stronger and more in control because they were trained to be. Others feel it is a bad rap, a stereotype that makes others perceive them as unapproachable. This is a real source of frustration for these professionals. When is it okay to speak up and take control? When, if ever, can the role of the "defenseless woman" be played? The following statements target these contradictions:

As lawyers from 9 to 7 in conflict one must be assertive. It's hard to change.

When one comes home, men want you to come in and take care of the children and step back—give up your control. Sometimes it is hard to give up control and put it in someone else's hands.

Because I am in control at work, I come home and hand over the control. When I was married, I would know answers to questions out there and back away. I couldn't directly tell him the answer. Then I'd pretend like he figured it out. It felt good doing it, but I did resent it. My husband couldn't deal with a woman in the driver's position.

Because of who we are and what we do, we voice our opinions to our mates. When they pick something to do and we don't like it, we speak up as opposed to going along *all* the time.

Another problem I have [is that] people always think you are being a "lawyer." You want answers and pull it out of them. You are being a lawyer. When you're pressing them they think you are being a lawyer. But we are trained and have a certain approach when it comes to getting answers.

You can sit back [in a relationship] but there comes a time when you want to speak out.

Initially you start out trying to be noncombative. But as you get more into the relationship, that changes.

The complaint that professional women change once they get into a relationship was felt to be bogus. The participants felt that most people change, not only professional black women:

[M]en are different, too. What you describe [professional women changing after they are in a relationship] is nothing unique to professional women. Women know how to eventually get that man to do what they want them to do. You know how to get him where you want them to be. My mother could do that and she just graduated from high school.

The issue of how African American men respond to high-powered women evoked a lot of emotion among the participants. The insecurity of many men regarding their ability to deal with an assertive, self-sufficient mate and the lack of African American men who are at their economic and educational level were two of the common complaints, as indicated in table 6.4.

Table 6.4
Greatest Barriers to Relationships

Respondent # L = Lawyer D = Doctor	Response
1L	Number of men who are not threatened
2L	The greatest barrier is our profession itself.
3L	Many men are too insecure to enter into a serious relationship with a woman who is intelligent and accomplished
4L	Availability of men; time and opportunity to meet them
5L	Black men who are emotionally distant and unable to commit
6L	Lack of quality men; men being intimidated by professional black women
7L	Insecurity of black men; scarcity of single black men in my social circle
1D	Changing perceptions regarding male/female roles coupled with racism
2D	Men's perception of professional women; everyone's perception of black women physicians as being all knowing
3D	Erroneous perception that professional black women feel "superior"
4D	Suitable mate
5D	Lack of choices

The issue of relationships is complicated for these professional women. Gender roles are indeed changing, but there still exists a constructed and rigid notion of what it means to be male or female (Hill Collins 1990). The professional woman has to respond to at least four issues. First, there is the battle of roles in a society where gender roles are changing for all people. Second, they are in a situation where societal messages are to find a mate of the same social stratum, and there are few black men who fit this criterion. Third, they are perceived as (and some really are) unapproachable, assertive, and controlling.

Fourth, they are in the strange quandary of power politics: some black men resent them because of the belief that the white man will allow a black woman to get ahead because black women are less threatening than black men:

Part of me agrees with that [black women are less threatening to white men], but I also think that a smart black woman can get close to the top of anything before anyone realizes it. If we were black men, we couldn't get there without fighting each step of the way.

When it comes down to the hierarchy, black women are at the bottom, no matter what type of status you have or don't have, for example look at Anita Hill. We are looked on as the glue of the family but we are still low on the totem pole.

Even in our positions we can manipulate things and we have a better chance than black men [because we are perceived as less threatening]. We have more potential.

[W]hite men don't perceive us as a threat or in competition with them. In terms of society, I feel society looks at black women as the lowest. Because of this, it's easier for us to get the education, job, etc. We are not as threatening.

Although there may be a consensus that black women are less threatening, these women are made to feel as if it is their fault that this quirk of racism exists (Giddings 1984). Should they not take the job? not get the education? Clearly, it would be ideal if black men and women could work together to uplift the community of African Americans. However, the battle of the sexes really strikes home when these professional women are held at fault for their desire for achievement and personal advancement in a society that just may view them as less threatening than black men.

Another issue confronting these women is that of the standard of beauty to which women are compared. One must keep in mind that these black professionals are all still playing on an uneven field, a field where white standards of beauty and "womanhood" are still considered to reign supreme. Our participants felt this was still the case as indicated by their comments regarding this standard:

White people look at beauty differently, all beautiful women are blond model types. The black people that tend to look beautiful to whites have white features, long hair, etc.

You are pretty if you have long hair, it's a given.

What also happens in our society is biased toward pretty people. Whatever pretty is defined as—these people are liked.

Prettiness is defined in the European way. It is like this even among black people.

We tend to choose the prettiest one. It's a prejudice we have in our society.

If you are dark you are never pretty.

I was in my late 20s before I thought I was attractive. I never had long hair, and I wasn't light. I grew up in the South where those features were favored. My saving grace was that I was smart.

I went to a local establishment, a club, with a friend. My friend was dark, with a wide nose and short hair. During the night, several men who looked like her stepped passed her to ask me to dance. I felt embarrassed for her to go through this and she said it happens all the time. Not one man said a word to her. With those men, African American features are so devalued. It is still perpetuated to young kids.

I went out with a man who said he was proud of himself because he never has gone out with a woman as dark as me.

I got over because I was smart. I think people are making more comments about color, now more than ever.

I thought at this point we would have left that black/white issue behind us. We, as blacks, don't work hard enough to reverse this process. We have to make an active effort to reverse this. For example, telling dark young girls with curly hair that they are beautiful.

There were a couple of dissenting voices:

I have friends with African features who are considered beautiful by white men even in professional settings.

They [whites] don't necessarily impose their standards of beauty. You can walk in with a short Afro and look beautiful to them.

Some researchers hypothesize that we are in a time where black features are "being erotocized" (Wade-Gayles 1984). However, the majority of the respondents still felt that we have not gotten past the issue of a white standard of beauty imposed on all people. They felt that black people have been so socialized into this mode of thinking that they are even more stringent with this standard of beauty. Thus, an African American professional woman with African features and dark skin is thought to have many strikes against her in the relationship game. Consequently, when asked about their greatest disappointment, five of the twelve participants answered with comments centered around not having a mate and/or children in their lives.

Based on the responses generated in the focus group, it was clear that these

African American female professionals felt that M.E.E.S. was a definite factor in their lives. When asked directly, "Do you think being a professional African American woman creates added stress for you?" the respondents unanimously answered yes. I attempted to disentangle the stress of gender from that of race by asking, "In your experiences which status creates the most stress for you: being African American, being in your profession, or being a woman?" Eight of the twelve responded being African American; four stated being a woman. Of these four, a couple also indicated that they could not disassociate one from another and marked both being African American and being female. Two indicated that their profession, coupled with being African American and female, all added to their stress. One respondent indicated that her answer would be different at different stages of her life, suggesting that she has grown accustomed to the stress of race over the years. It has indeed become very mundane.

In the focus groups, participants acknowledged their feelings of gratitude for being able to have the concept of M.E.E.S. articulated and discussed. One respondent took the concept and came up with a formula for her stellar achievements:

Super performance = M.E.E.S.   X   Confidence.

SUCCESS AND STRATEGIES FOR COPING WITH M.E.E.S.

Table 6.5
Greatest Joys

Respondent # L = Lawyer D = Doctor	Response
1L	No response
2L	Learning to appreciate myself and my self-worth
3L	Music, achieving goals
4L	My grandparents; passing the bar
5L	Graduation from law school; wedding day
6L	The advancement of blacks as a people; my professional accomplishment; my mother
7L	Friends and family
1D	Music, career, golf
2D	Patients seem satisfied or happy with my performance
3D	Comforting and reassuring patients; pleasing others
4D	Completing residency and becoming a surgeon
5D	Caribbean vacations

Although much of the discussion in the focus groups centered on the stresses of black female professionals, each group was very upbeat. It was clear that these women receive great joy from their accomplishments. When asked about their greatest joys, I received the responses listed in Table 6.5. Achieving their goals, helping others, family, and doing things to show self-appreciation summarize these joys. Success in the professional arena has allowed our respondents to have a sense of independence and control over certain aspects of their lives. Dr. Chester Pierce (1969) has stated that the way to decrease mundane extreme environmental stress is to increase four life variables: skill, autonomy, safety (both physical and psychological), and purposeful interaction with others. These black professional women have been very successful at getting to the top of the skill spectrum, which has afforded them a sense of autonomy. They live in physically safe neighborhoods and have the material luxuries that high incomes make possible. The previous section details how psychological safety is not always as easily purchased or readily available. Almost intuitively, these women thrive on purposeful interaction with others. This is strongly suggested in their responses to the question, "When you want to celebrate success or personal achievement, what do you normally do?" Each response focused on sharing with close friends and family. By their responses to the focus group, however, I believe that they would welcome greater opportunities to "purposely interact" around issues that affect their lives. Merely talking about such issues and getting them out in the open are satisfying and stress reducing for some.

Sharing coping strategies was also a helpful exercise according to the participants. They varied from self-indulging activities to exercise as described in table 6.6.

Many of our participants indicated that it is hard to relax, given their workloads. One stated that there were periods in her life where she "didn't know how to have a good time." Another stated:

I have a real hard time doing nothing. I don't know how to relax because I am always used to going, going, going. When doing nothing, I become guilty because of the things I should be doing.

Although very stressful on many fronts, these participants agreed that they would do it over again—as far as choosing their profession. There was a general feeling of satisfaction and accomplishment among the participants. The following responses are indicative of the feeling of the group:

[There is a] self-satisfaction of achieving your goal—the level of respect in the community, and greater community; people across the board respond differently to you. I even do it myself—a whole different perspective.

There is a certain standing you have in the community. Because of the economic class it puts us in; we are now exposed to various opportunities.

I don't have any regrets right now. I'm enjoying myself even though I am not married and have no children.

I have learned to appreciate myself and my accomplishment.   Longevity gives a certain amount of security.

The respondents were not saying that they would not change anything in their professional development, only that they would still choose the same profession. Some shared the changes they would make if they had to do it over again, such as choice of medical specialty:

I would be a physician [do it over again].   There are few things that afford this income. In terms of change, I would have chosen a different school because being in predominately white schools and communities affected my social life.   You have to give more direction to your social life and not leave it up to chance.

I would go into medicine but pick another specialty.   I didn't have counseling about lifestyle choices other than that I'm all right.   I would think about the long haul more.

Table 6.6
Coping Strategies

Respondent # L = Lawyer D = Doctor	Response/Strategies
1L	Exercise; talking with friends
2L	Talking the situation through with close friends; my boyfriend and some close girlfriends
3L	Prayer and exercise; talking with family and friends
4L	I don't have good coping strategies
5L	Denial; exercise
6L	Talking with close friends; spend time to "get away"
7L	Prayer and talking with friends
1D	Music, sleep, sports
2D	Reading self-help books
3D	Reassessing and reflecting within myself; reassuring self-worth
4D	Pray and talk to friends
5D	Eating

I confess, talking with these women gave me a very strong sense of pride in the strength, persistence, and accomplishment of black women.   They are indeed standing in stellar spaces: surgeons, a pediatric cardiologist, partners in major law firms, specialists in a variety of domains. At times, the stress of feeling that you are "out in space" by yourself can be overwhelming. Juggling around issues of being African American, a professional in control, and a woman with needs for companionship can be at times exhilarating and at times depressing. However, one of the major ways these women cope, and succeed, is by being able to use other black women as their support system. The Black Women Physicians and Black Women Lawyers professional organizations provide a forum for discussion and community service. Friendship networks between and among these two groups serve as a foundation for "purposeful interaction," both in words and deeds. Further study of success and what indexes promote the use of M.E.E.S. as a motivational factor versus a debilitation must be conducted to help define and develop strategies. These women are forging the path for those who come after them.   It is important that young African American girls see that there are role models for them, thanks to the efforts of stellar women such as these.

7

Summary

A white policeman yelled, "Hey, boy! Come here!" Somewhat
bothered, I retorted: "I'm no boy!" He then rushed at me, in-
flamed, and stood towering over me, snorting, "What d'ja say,
boy? Quickly he frisked me and demanded, "What's your name,
boy?" Frightened, I replied, "Dr. Poussaint, I'm a physician." He
angrily chuckled and hissed, "What's your first name, boy?" When
I hesitated he assumed a threatening stance and clinched his fists.
As my heart palpitated, I muttered in profound humiliation,
"Alvin."

He continued his psychological brutality, bellowing, "Alvin,
the next time I call you, you come right away, you hear? You
hear?" I hesitated. "You hear me, boy?"

Dr. Alvin Poussaint (1971)

In the last semester of my son's senior year of high school, he asked to talk with
me. I had no problems with talking to my son, Tajai. We talk regularly.
However, he had this expression on his face that made me think that he had
something quite serious to say. He began the conversation by telling me that he
had called some of the many schools to which he had been admitted for college.
I was quite proud that he had gotten into every school to which he applied, including those private ones that white folks think black folks are underqualified
to get into, such as Harvard, Princeton, Yale, and Stanford. He had called a few
of the schools to see if they would defer his admission if he chose to stay out of
school for a year. This caught my attention. What did he mean, stay out of
school for a year!?! He went on to say that his "rap" group was offered a contract with Jive Records and that he wanted to spend the next year pursuing this
rap career. I don't know if I heard much of what he said after that—something
about needing me to sign a contract since he was only seventeen and that the
stepfather of one of the group members was the attorney handling the group.
Jive records, what's up with *that* name? I tried to keep a poker face and not let
my son see that I was going crazy on the inside. I wanted him to think that he
had a rational mother who understood his burning desire to rap. I wanted him to

feel empowered to make decisions about his life as he began the journey to adulthood. Yet, I knew I could not handle this request at this time. I got it together enough to tell him that I had to go do something and that we would continue the discussion tomorrow. I then left because I knew that if I stayed in his eye view much longer, he would know that I was beginning to unravel.

I thought about my son's request for the rest of the day. He was an above 4.0 student and over the years of his development, I knew he would be going to college after high school graduation. I had not even entertained the thought that he would take a year off—I didn't even like rap at that time. I thought about how I was proud of my son, not only because of his intellect but also because he was an all around good kid: gregarious, kind, sensitive, and in possession of a strong sense of self. He was indeed "black and proud." Then I wondered, What was it that made me have such a strong emotional reaction to his request to stay out of school for a year? It wasn't only because of the desire to be a rap artist. I knew he had had a love of rap for years. He was a wonderful poet, and this was a positive avenue for him to do something he loved. As I thought about my di- lemma, I realized that this was one of the most difficult battles I had encountered with the M.E.E.S. factor. It hit me like a hammer. I was extremely stressed because I knew that my son would be subjugated to stereotypes, negative judg- ments, and potential physical abuse in the real world just because he was an Af- rican American male. School, although not perfect, was in my mind at least a partial refuge from the reality of day-to-day life in a racist society because in the academic environment, racism is often handled intellectually. I knew he could combat the intellectual battles. I worried about the physical ones.

I thought about the story Dr. Alvin Poussaint (1971) tells about the time he got stopped by the white police officer, which opened this chapter. I also thought about the many times my son had gotten stopped by police officers for no reason at all on his way home. They didn't expect a black boy with dread- locks to be walking or driving the streets in a nice neighborhood. It didn't mat- ter that Dr. Poussaint was an eminent psychiatrist and author or that my son was an "A" student on his way to Stanford University. They were seen as black men, potential dangers to the white establishment.

One of the legacies of our history in these United States is the relationship between individual racism and institutional racism, which gets played out in situations like those just described. This relationship is a central part of M.E.E.S. Policemen have the blessings of the institution to "serve and pro- tect." However, who they serve and protect often becomes an individual call. Surely, you might say that the laws are there for everyone to follow, that they are colorblind. If this were true, how do we interpret the disproportionate num- ber of African Americans who are stopped and arrested, the disproportionate number of African Americans receiving stiffer sentences than whites for similar crimes, and the disproportionate number of African Americans in prison and on death row (Carroll 1974; Debro 1977; Nelson 1992; Blumstein 1995)? I firmly believe that laws are unevenly applied. It is that curious mix of individuals socialized to believe that "Black = Bad" and the institutions that have been too frequently used to protect and serve the power relationships of the status quo. This adds significantly to the daily stress that accompanies being black. African Americans must be constantly vigilant about their behavior because Dr. Poussaint's case was not an isolated one, but one that is repeated daily.

A more common example of how laws depend on an individual's judgment to implement them is seen when you are driving on an interstate highway or freeway. You know that most of the drivers are going above the speed limit. How does the highway patrol officer make the decision about whom to stop and give a ticket? What triggers him or her to pursue and pull over a driver for a common speeding ticket? The patrol officer is given the institutional power to make this decision, as he or she cannot stop all of the speeders. As you are stopped and watch all of the other cars speed by, as a black person, you do entertain the thought that you were stopped because the patrol person saw that you were black. This example of M.E.E.S. may seem trivial, but I thought about all of the system-condoned ways that could get to, deter, and derail my son, and I had a panic attack when he wanted to take a year off to rap. I guess I mistakenly thought that a college degree would better shield him against the microaggressions he would have to confront. I again thought of Dr. Poussaint's experience. His degrees did not shield him. The desire to have my son go for what he loved and feel empowered to make a life decision forced me to overcome my fear of his inability to handle the M.E.E.S. factor. I talked with him the next day. I shared my concerns, but I told him I would support his decision if he promised me he would return to school in a year. He made the promise, and he kept it.

Later that summer, I read, *Days of Grace*, an autobiography of Arthur Ashe (Ashe and Rampersad 1993). I admired the quiet dignity of Arthur Ashe, and wondered what he would have said to my son. He had written:

It [segregation] left me a marked man, forever aware of the shadow of contempt that lay across my identity and my sense of self-esteem. I don't want to overstate the case, I think of myself, and others think of me, as supremely self-confident. Still, I also know that the shadow is always there; only death will free me, and blacks like me, from its pall.

I knew that like Arthur Ashe, my son had high self-esteem and was extremely self-confident. Arthur Ashe's life was cut short due to the deadly disease, AIDS. In a TV special he shared:

[I]t is harder to live as a black in America than it has been having AIDS. It has been time consuming and wasteful.[1]

---

[1] This statement was taken from a Home Box Office special celebrating the life and accomplishments of Arthur Ashe. It was aired in 1994.

I thought about Arthur Ashe's battle with AIDS and his battle in life to be dignified, and walk tall as an African American man.   I had been second-guessing my decision to let Tajai stay out of school a year, but my readings and reflections about Arthur Ashe helped me to build a sense of confidence in Tajai's decision. No African American can escape the shadow of living in a society that still views blackness with contempt.   No person can escape the cards that life deals. Thus, I felt I should encourage my son to go for his dream; take the risk; empower himself.   This seemed to be a viable response to living in the shadow.

RESPONSE   MODES

As indicated by the responses shared by the many study participants in these chapters, African Americans respond to the day-to-day stress brought on by being black in a variety of ways.   The adaptability of African Americans constantly amazes me.   Given our history in this country, the constant abuse, and perpetuation of the "Black = Bad" equation, it is a testimony of our strength that has allowed African Americans to survive and, in many cases, thrive in such a context.   This is not to say that all of us are thriving.   There are response modes that are extremely useful and productive, such as those employed by the successful single fathers, doctors, and lawyers represented in the preceding case studies. However, there are also response modes that can be described as maladaptive. Many young people have given up hope for the future and daily engage in life-threatening behavior.   These young people are frequently seen on the TV tabloids but, more often, they are quiet victims of M.E.E.S. and are on the rolls of the many negative statistics: percent more likely to be homicide victims; percent less likely to finish high school; percent overrepresented in prison; percent more likely to die of cancer, high blood pressure, and a variety of other physical illnesses.

There are indeed many ways one lives with being African American in this society.   The following response modes incorporate this spectrum:

Overachievement

As indicated by the stories of the professional women in chapter 6, the single fathers in chapter 2 and the mothers of the toddlers in chapter 4, many African Americans believe that in order to be successful in the context of racism, they have to be better than whites.   They feel that they have to be twice as good to get the same privileges.   There is a realization and understanding that African Americans are still the targets of racism and consequently lower expectations. For example, one of the physicians stated that she got angry when her high school counselor pushed her toward technical school and pushed the white students (some with lesser grades and abilities) toward college.   She channeled this anger into achievement.   She wanted to show the counselor and those who did not appreciate her talents that she could go to college, could excel, and could become a doctor. Many autobiographical stories of African Americans who have excelled show that they have done so partly because they had to prove themselves on an uneven playing field. Although this response mode can yield substantial professional results, it, too, can have liabilities. I am sure there are countless stories of African Americans who push themselves to exhaustion and still are not able to reap the fair rewards for their work.

Ignore/Suppress

The difficulty in acknowledging that being black creates a set of obstacles that are beyond one's control is, at times, overwhelming. Many African Americans close their eyes to this—a means of avoidance. They ignore or suppress the micro-aggressions. They try not to get upset when subtle issues of racism come up and often try to explain it away (i.e., the salesperson just didn't see that I was next). As one of the parents in chapter 4 states, "with me, I ignore it most of the time. I just ignore it." For some this strategy is a lifesaver because they feel if they cannot ignore or suppress it, they would be spending all of their waking hours fighting, getting angry, or just being frustrated at the system. A critical skill is knowing when to ignore and when to fight back. This is a most stressing problem for some African Americans, as fighting back is frequently time consuming and often puts one in harm's way. For example, a colleague of mine shared that his son, a college student, was recently arrested because he was bold enough to ask a police officer why he was being hassled. He was taking pictures of a building for a class assignment. The officer arrested him. M.E.E.S. is invoked as both my colleague and his son do not believe this would have happened to a young white college student trying to get his assignment completed. Time in jail and in court, anger, attorney fees, and so forth, can all be part of the cost of "fighting back." On the other hand, loss of self-respect can be a very heavy price for ignoring many such micro-aggressions. One of our case study mothers stated, "You have to know what things you can 'shine on' and what things you should fight for."

Self-Devaluation

As a result of believing the constant barrage of negativity that confronts African Americans, some incorporate this negativity into their own sense of self. This is supported by the symbolic interactionist theory that opened this volume. People who have incorporated the generalized others' negative point of view of blackness and have experienced firsthand negativity because of their blackness can really suffer from self-devaluation. They have not been provided positive mediators who challenge the stereotype, or who help them in deciphering the truth from myth in the depiction of African Americans. They have not had positive role models to help them nullify the effect of the "Black = Bad" equation. They frequently do not have "traditional" avenues to positively channel their time, space, or energy in productive ways. Consequently, they often engage in self-destructive behavior and have very little self-value. When a case study mother stated that being black "might make some feel they have an inferiority complex," she is sharing her concern for the children who believe the racist propaganda against African Americans. When people think lowly of themselves, they do not expect much of themselves, and thus, they are less likely to be disappointed. This may serve to buffer the pain; however, low expectations can become self-fulfilling prophecies: no expectations, thus no disappointment, thus no success, thus perpetuation of self-devaluation and stereotype.

Anti-White

As a result of feeling constantly harassed and being treated unfairly by those considered controllers of the power structure (which translates to white people for many African Americans), some blacks truly take a strong anti-white stance. They do not want to associate with whites and believe that whites represent the devil or all that is evil. This was stated in chapter 4 when a mother said that the stress related to being black "makes them have a chip on their shoulder and be mad all of the time and hate white folks. It do!" Many African Americans from across all class and economic lines have a very strong dislike for whites in general, even though they might have white friends. Whites frequently talk about blacks who they befriend as being "exceptions" to the "typical" African Americans they see depicted on TV. This rationale is also used by African Americans who feel that the "good whites" are exceptions based on an assumption that taken collectively whites are evil.

Pro-Black

Often anti-white and pro-black response modes get lumped together. However, there is a difference. Many African Americans believe that they have to overly support blacks in order to help deflect and make up for the history of racism. Some believe that identifying with one's own ethnic/cultural group is very positive and natural. This does not automatically imply anti-white. It does lead some to associate less with whites, but the emphasis is on a more internal self-love stance. Thus, there were a couple of parents in our samples (both the TIES sample and the single fathers sample) who felt strongly that their children should have black service providers, black dolls, and other positive black images in their environment. In chapter 2, one father sums up his feelings on this issue by stating, "When black kids look at their history, they only see the negative, they think slavery is their culture. I think it is important that black kids be taught, not European history, but African history. They'll see the richness and want to do something. Perhaps we can get them away from the 'what is there to live for' attitude."

The necessity to separate fact from fiction in the presentation of history is a common theme for those who engage in this response mode. A belief that black children are lied to in schools, in the media, and in various other institutions makes it necessary to set the record straight. In so doing, black children are able to better combat and resist the popular negative images they encounter daily. Adults who engage in this response mode frequently surround themselves with others who share their views. This creates an environment where one can have more "psychological safety"—where the micro-aggressions that too commonly accompany black/white interactions are avoided.   Many professional African Americans are daily in a work environment where they must interact with European Americans. They have little control of this in the professional arena. However, many state that they have more control of their social arena and prefer that those with whom they socialize be African American.

Identify with the Oppressor

Some African Americans truly believe that they can be more successful and live better lives if they just become more white. They adopt the philosophy encouraged by the media and white power structure regarding the reason most blacks are part of the negative statistics: because of their laziness and lack of ability. This response mode often carries with it a denial of the historical and current manifestations of racism. It also produces blacks who often espouse the traditional white views more eloquently and voraciously than whites do. Black men such as Judge Clarence Thomas, University of California regent Ward Connerly, and San Jose State professor Shelby Steele are examples of men who espouse a very conservative (some even consider it anti-black) political stance, who married white women, and who are frequently given tremendous media exposure for their "pull yourself up by your bootstraps"—you can make it if you just try; I made it why can't you; we are all on a level playing field now—view. These views are consistent with those of people perceived to be in control of our institutions. Blacks who espouse them are often given special treatment by politicians, academicians, and the media. On the other hand, they are frequently thought of with disdain among the larger African American communities.

Anger and Rage

The micro-aggressions that occur daily in the lives of African Americans do not go unrecognized. Anger and rage frequently accompany them. Sometimes this anger and rage is controllable and other times it is not. Shortly after I began my work at U.C. Berkeley, I received a call from a student service provider. She informed me that one of my African American female students just went "crazy" in the middle of campus. The student was screaming at all those passing by, and had to be calmed down. I spoke with the student and she shared that she had been taking snide comments all semester, particularly that morning. She knew they were racially motivated and was just "pissed off" at white people. She was a good student and generally very even tempered. I knew that she needed counseling. The irony was that the student counseling center wanted her to see a white therapist. This was the last thing that this young student needed to do in her mental state! The anger and rage need to be released at times. This may occur when one least expects it. It is like that "last straw on the camel's back." Micro-aggressions can be kept in and the anger can be building. Depending on the circumstances, a comment, a stare, an accidental bumping in passing can lead to an opportunity for release. Research indicates that spouse abuse and child abuse are linked to anger and rage that cannot be directed at their primary targets (Barton and Baglio 1993; Hamberger and Renzetti 1996). The other side of the coin is represented by the many cases where disgruntled former employees come back and shoot their employers. They feel they are getting even with those responsible for their anger and rage.

Most African Americans use acceptable channels to release their anger and rage—such as over-achievement, humor, or religion. Others can be quite violent in their release modes. One TIES parent felt that "some of us say that we're dealing with it by verbally abusing each other, verbally and physically. Nowadays you hear of a lot of black suicide and you didn't use to hear that." The anger and rage can get turned inwardly and lead to self-destructive behavior such as we see in street gangs (drive-by shootings, drug use, abuse of women). Channeling the anger and rage can be a very difficult task.

Hopelessness

One of the most common responses to M.E.E.S. and the status of being black, combined with many of the consequences thereof, is hopelessness. There are some African Americans who are truly beaten down. They feel apathetic and hopeless regarding their own self-empowerment in addition to the collective empowerment of blacks. One of our mothers describes this hopelessness when she talks of her husband who now "won't fight. He'll just take it, whereas before, he used to be the one that would fight for it. Now they done did it to him so many times, he won't fight. He just says, well that's the way it is." The psychological research literature is replete with studies on the negative effects of hopelessness. Jesse Jackson's mantra, "Keep hope alive," is also a testimonial to the importance of having hope in our communities. Although Professor Derrick Bell is personally a very hopeful man, even his story (which opened this volume) speaks of hopelessness. The mere fact that whites would gladly trade African Americans to space traders implies that this country would prefer to not deal with blacks. This is not a hopeful sign of the times.

These response modes are not developmental, not hierarchical, not mutually exclusive. African Americans can engage in any of these responses at any given time, depending on the circumstances. We can also change from one predominant mode of response to another if our circumstances change. Irrespective of which response modes are adopted, there is one clear and consistent thread that is stitched across all of these response modes: they create added stress on the lives of those who must engage in them. Whether we embrace our blackness or reject it, the fact that we must deal with "it" within a context of devalued group status creates stress. The recent medical literature on the disproportionate number of African Americans suffering from high blood pressure or hypertension (leading to strokes and heart attacks), diabetes, and cancer can be linked to stress. Holding our frustrations on the inside, not knowing why we feel so upset, or even feeling guilty about issues as they relate to race can take a serious toll, both medically and psychologically. Jill Nelson, Ph.D. (1993) put this eloquently when she described her experience doing the "standard Negro balancing act":

I've been doing the standard Negro balancing act when it comes to dealing with white folks, which involves sufficiently blurring the edges of my being so that white folks don't feel intimidated and simultaneously holding on to my integrity, there is a thin line between Uncle Tomming and Mau-Mauing. To step over that line can mean disaster. On one side lies employment and self-hatred, on the other, the equally dubious honor of unemployment with integrity. In the middle lies something like employment with honor, although I'm not sure exactly how that works.

As the teen moms, doctors, lawyers, employed single fathers, parents, and students in this volume tell us, the micro-aggressions associated with M.E.E.S. are not bound to age, class, or circumstance for African Americans. The inner-city ghetto youth must confront policemen who believe them all to be thieves, thugs, and gang members. Many of these youth live in depressing and perceived hopeless environments. Such stories are told regularly in the news, on TV, and in movies such as *New Jack City, Strapped, Menace to Society, South Central,* and *Set It Off.* The anger of the youth, their sense of hopelessness, and their lack of respect for life is clearly depicted. However, one should be clear, the anger is not bound by the borders of the ghetto. Attorney Patricia Williams (1991) described a micro-aggression in just trying to shop for a Christmas gift for her mother:

I was shopping in Soho and saw in a store window a sweater that I wanted to buy for my mother. I pressed my round brown face to the window and my finger on the buzzer, seeking admittance. A narrow-eyed, white teenager wearing running shoes and feasting on bubble gum glared out, evaluating me for signs that would pit me against the limits of his social understanding. After about five seconds, he mouthed, "We're closed," and blew pink rubber at me. It was two Saturdays before Christmas, at one o'clock in the afternoon; there were several white people in the store who appeared to be shopping for things for their mothers. I was enraged.

The difference between the micro-aggressions faced by ghetto youth and depicted in the movies and the experience described by Patricia Williams may seem large.

Their age, their gender, their economic and educational backgrounds are quite different. However, their communality often gets overlooked: both must face micro-aggressions due to their black and brown skins; most of these micro-aggressions are beyond their control; most cause stress on the recipients; and most lead to frustration and anger. Due to Williams's educational background and her sense of empowerment within the system, she was able to write about this experience and release some of her anger. On the contrary, young men who do not have these advantages may take less socially accepted routes to ease their frustration, too often leading to incarceration and death. It is to the advantage of society to have educated, articulate, and personally empowered citizens, citizens who feel they have a stake in society and therefore will work within an acceptable framework. Many African Americans have chosen to work within the system. Some have done exceedingly well despite racism. However, a growing number of our young are choosing dangerous response modes in their fight to cope with M.E.E.S. It is time to address the cause of maladaptive behavior, the cause of self-devaluation, the cause of anger, the cause of mundane extreme environmental stress.

Decreasing the racism that causes M.E.E.S. is the major and most desired step in the right direction. This will not happen overnight, if at all. Thus, strategies need to be created for helping one combat M.E.E.S. As we have learned from previous chapters, research and media are focused far more on the negative in relationship to African Americans than on the positive. A closer look at strategies for successfully negotiating M.E.E.S. is warranted. We need to learn from our successes and see if we can adopt methods that we can use to teach others to be successful.

The following strategies were extracted from the data presented in this volume and the experiences of those who shared their stories in this volume. They are not definitive. However, the dialogue focusing on successfully negotiating M.E.E.S. must begin with those who daily experience the micro-aggressions that by definition accompany M.E.E.S. The African Americans whose voices are heard in the preceding pages are informants. They have shared their world, their personal encounters, their hopes and fears. Hopefully, these testimonies and resulting strategies can serve to facilitate this dialogue.

STRATEGIES TO BUFFER M.E.E.S.

The responses listed in the previous section describe the psychological response modes of reacting to M.E.E.S. To survive and thrive as a community, African Americans and concerned others must discuss, develop, and implement strategies to move our sometimes maladaptive behavior to more positive action in our struggle to cope with M.E.E.S. In previous chapters there have been discussions about many of the strategies. Setting positive examples, role modeling, networking, planning, persistence, and self-love have all been suggested as strategies in which we can engage to positively impact our children and communities. There are a few other strategies that I would like to emphasize in summary.

First, the problems surrounding the issues discussed in this volume and the resulting stress for African Americans (ME.E.S.) have to be acknowledged. In our desire to be considered equal and seen for the content of our character, we too often try to ignore that racism still exists. We also try to ignore and hide its negative consequences on all of us. When we suppress racism, it eats away at us slowly. Accurate historical as well as current information about African Americans must be understood. This information must also be shared with our children in appropriate contexts. If we, as loving and concerned parents, do not present, screen, and interpret information for our children, they are left with what others tell them and their own immediate experience. This is without the benefit of contextualization from someone with more experience with racism and who has their best interest at heart. An example of how this contextualization is so critical for positive development is seen in the following true scenario, which was shared with me by a friend:

> A few winters ago, a young mother took her daughter to buy a coat. They found a coat they liked in a store which had a common dressing room, a large room with mirrored walls and where everyone could see everyone else. When they approached the dressing room, a saleswoman who was at the door looked at them and told them that they would have to take off their coats before going in to try on the new coat. The mother saw that there were many in the dressing room with their own coats as well as the new coats with them. The daughter saw this too and was perplexed. The mother knew that the woman was engaging in racist behavior The mother and her daughter were the only black patrons. The mother saw the look on her daughter's face. She told her daughter, "Honey, this woman thinks that black people steal and that is why she wants us to leave *our* coats and why she didn't ask the white people to leave *their* coats with her. We know that we do not steal any more than whites do, and this woman has a *big* problem. You can make the decision. Should we buy a coat here where they hire whites with such problems or do you think we should look somewhere else?" The mother spoke clearly and loudly so that all the other patrons heard her statements. The patrons all looked toward the saleswoman. They, too, were beginning to feel embarrassed. The saleswoman turned red and started stammering about how they must not have understood what she said and that they didn't have to leave their coats with her.

In this example, the mother empowered her daughter by turning a situation around which could have been psychologically damaging to her daughter. The daughter had clarity. The problem was the saleswoman, not her. The issue was racism. It was acknowledged and addressed in a manner which served to empower, not confuse, the daughter.

Another effective strategy to combat M.E.E.S. is to equip ourselves and our children with knowledge and wisdom regarding the history of Africans and African Americans. There have been so many myths, lies, and fabrications that most African Americans have little accurate knowledge of the contributions of Africans and African Americans to the world. Accurate information can serve to filter the inaccurate data. It can also serve to help build healthy self-concepts. The history of African Americans did not start with slavery. Blacks are not disproportionately in jail or out of school because we are lazy and like to break laws. Just because a story is written in a history book or in a professional journal does not make it true. Dr. Gresham's (1989) citations in chapter 1 clearly articulate how history books and other pseudoacademic works are often intentionally spreading misinformation to support the political views of the status quo. An example of how accurate data can be used as a filter is seen in the following experience of a black high school student.

> In a local history high school class, the teacher was presenting how the United States was fortunate in that it had never been bombed on its mainland during conflict. She described the bombing at Pearl Harbor and the massive bombing of our allies during World War Two. One young African American student suggested that this was not true. He shared with the class that in 1921, Tulsa, Oklahoma was bombed from the air. This happened during a race riot and many black people were killed by other U.S. citizens. The teacher had never heard this and questioned the young man about the validity of his comment. He came in the next day and brought a copy of the following article dated March 13, 1983 authored by Irving Wallace, David Wallechinshy and Amy Wallace. It was titled "First U.S. City to be Bombed from the Air." I include it because this is the type of information that we do not see reflected in the history books:

>> *In 1921, during one of the worse race riots in American history, Tulsa, Oklahoma became the first U.S. city to be bombed from the air. More than 75 persons — mostly blacks — were killed.*
>>
>> *Before the riot, Tulsa blacks were so successful that their business district was called "The Negro's Wall Street." Envy bred hatred of the blacks who accounted for a tenth of the segregated city's population of 100,000.*
>>
>> *Then on May 30, 1921, a white female elevator*

operator accused Dick Rowland, a 19-year-old black who worked at a shoeshine stand, of attacking her. Though he denied the charge, Rowland was jailed. The Tulsa Tribune ran a sensational account of the incident the next day and a white lynch mob soon gathered at the jail. Armed blacks seeking to pro- tect Rowland also showed up. Someone fired a gun, and the riot was on.

Whites invaded the black district, burning, loot- ing and killing. To break up the riot, the police commandeered private planes and dropped dynamite. Eventually, the National Guard was called in and martial law declared.

The police arrested more than 4000 blacks and interned them in three camps. All blacks were forced to carry green ID cards. And when Tulsa was zoned for a new railroad station, the tracks were routed through the black business district, thus destroying it.

More recently, in the *San Francisco Chronicle*, April 9, 1994, an article entitled "Massacre survivors to be compensated" was published. This article described how the Florida Legislature agreed to pay up to $150,000 each to survivors of a "week long rampage by a white mob that wiped out the black town of Rosewood 71 years ago." In this incident at least eight people died and "nearly every house and building in the Gulf Coast community was burned." Once again this inci- dent was triggered because whites failed to find a black man who was accused of assaulting a white woman. It is of critical importance in our battle against M.E.E.S. that we have the knowledge tools to fight inaccurate portrayals of Af- rican Americans. Much of the truth is buried, rewritten, and is not presented in the appropriate context for understanding the larger issues of racism.

Consistent with increasing our knowledge, Dr. Pierce (1969) suggests that African Americans must increase four dimensions of our lives to reduce M.E.E.S.: our skill levels; our autonomy; our physical and psychological safety; and our purposeful interaction with others. Many black parents and grandparents echoed the need to be highly skilled when they told their children, "You have to be twice as good as whites in order to get ahead." Too often in corporate and other institutional settings, those in control use skills and other certifications as barriers for African Americans. Skills are needed to get the job done; however, a willing employer can provide opportunities for those he or she chooses to support. Many stories of not getting a position or a career advance- ment and then learning that the person who did get the prize was white and "less qualified" are shared at dinner tables throughout the African American commu- nity. Was the person really less qualified? Did race really matter? If all things were equal, would you have gotten the job? These questions are not always easy to answer. The mere fact that African Americans must think about them in so many areas is a M.E.E.S. factor. According to Pierce, one way to get more clarity is to build strong skills. If you know you are skilled, then you know you have other options and will not have to question this aspect of your portfolio.

Autonomy is also important. Dr. Julianne Malveaux (1994), an economist, discussed how many people may have good jobs but no autonomy. She stated that when one has bills to pay, a family to care for, and no fiscal security other than the monthly pay check, one is wearing "golden handcuffs." A person in this position cannot risk any behavior that might put his or her job at risk. Thus, the person may be at risk of not being able to "fight back" when the micro-aggressions on the job become psychologically trying. Autonomy is a goal that many will never reach; however, it is a goal for which we can strive. We can work to rid ourselves of the "golden handcuffs."

Physical and psychological safety are also elusive. The need for physical safety is obvious. We must teach our children that there really is physical danger in some settings. Equally important, for psychological safety, children must know why situations are dangerous. They must be able to get help and support in developing strategies to avoid these situations. Without this understanding and support, many young African Americans are socialized to be afraid of African Americans. This just serves to perpetuate the "Black = Bad" equation and adds to the negative psychological state this equation fosters.

When Pierce suggests we engage in more purposeful interaction, he is not referring to the mundane "how is the weather?" type of conversations. Stress is reduced when people interact with one another in a meaningful manner. This assumes that discussions are about important issues, issues about which people care and want to share. This is consistent with our sample doctors and lawyers, who emphasized the importance of friends. Social networking, friendship circles, and other mechanisms where African Americans can discuss important issues, feel valued and understood, are essential tools to combat M.E.E.S. Pierce has conducted research in the Arctic that underscores the importance of this type of support. A battery of medical and psychological tests were taken on those participating in the Iditarod, a major sled race that takes tremendous endurance under extremely harsh conditions. After the race, the data analyses indicated that family support was a key predictor of successful completion. The environment in which African Americans live, work, and play can also be harsh and require great endurance, according to Pierce. Accordingly, these findings in the extreme environment of the Arctic have relevance in our M.E.E.S. discussions. African Americans truly need to have a support network to be successful.

One of the deleterious side effects of M.E.E.S. described in chapter 5 is the suppression of one's willingness to take risks. Our U.C. Berkeley students were often reluctant to ask questions in class or make comments. They believed that by asking something that might be considered "silly or stupid," the rest of the class and the professor would just confirm their beliefs that black students are not qualified to be on the campus. Asking the question would be taking the risk that the question was valid or that the professor cared and did not buy into the stereotype. Our TIES study parents were also fearful of letting their young children take risks because they knew that the world was not supportive of African American children. When one reads the autobiographies of very successful people, the one major variable that goes across all of their stories is the fact that they took risks. The dilemma for us becomes how do we develop risk-taking skills and still provide physical and psychological safety? We definitely need more research on viable answers to this question.

Prior to conducting the TIES interviews and observations, I was involved in pilot testing some of the methodology we would use. An observation with a father and his three-year-old son suggested to me that risk-taking behavior can be developed very early with our children. The three-year-old was playing with an airplane that had round slots for the people in the plane. There were passenger, pilot, and copilot slots carved into the plane. The people were wooden with painted faces, clothing, and so forth, and they all fit into the round slots. There was only one brown-faced figure in the collection of ten to twelve figures. This one brown figure was painted with a pair of slacks and shirt. The pilot and copilot had blue uniforms. The young boy put all of the figures in the slots. The father pulled the brown-faced figure out of his passenger slot. He said, "This is a really good looking young man. He looks a bit like you. I bet he is really smart like you." His son smiled. The father picked up the pilot from his pilot's slot. He then switched the two figures, putting the brown-faced figure into the pilot's seat. He said, "I think that this young man (the brown-faced figure) is so smart he can be the pilot of the airplane." The son protested. He told his father that the young man did not have on the pilot's uniform. The father said with a smile, "Son, you don't have to have the uniform to do the job well." This satisfied the son and they continued playing with the African American in the pilot's seat. I share this story because it has many important messages: the African American figure is like us; the African American is smart; and, you don't have to look the part to play the part. However, the most important message I gained from this story is that of the father teaching his son to take the risk of doing things differently. Just because the designers of the game put the uniform on the white figure does not mean that we have to play the game accordingly. You can take the risk on the African American pilot and it will be fine because he is smart like you. Self-confidence, skill, and many of the aforementioned variables can and do serve as a viable foundation for productive risk taking. One also must feel comfortable: if the risk is taken and I am unsuccessful, there is still a safety net upon which to land. Weaving in this safety net is a major challenge for our families and communities and will help in our constant M.E.E.S. struggles.

Physical health is also an important issue in our struggle. Our communities boast the greatest athletes in the world. Our children know who their favorite players are and emulate them. These players have been marketed well on TV.

In most of our communities, they have greater name recognition than any of our historical heroes or local African American community leaders. They have been marketed to make money for many corporations and they command huge salaries. One of the marketing strategies that has not been mounted as strongly, however, is in the area of health. A great athlete is generally a physically healthy person. In the African American community, many factors mitigate physical as well as psychological well-being. M.E.E.S., like any type of stress, can have a major negative impact on one's physical health. Weight issues, smoking, lack of exercise, eating the wrong types of food, and alcohol and drug abuse are all activities in which one can engage to avoid and suppress M.E.E.S. On the other hand, they are each also factors that can and inevitably do compound the negative effects of M.E.E.S. Being healthy adds to our endurance and our physical safety. Health is an important thread in our "safety net" and should be considered a priority if we are serious in our struggle to reduce M.E.E.S.

For many, spirituality and a connection to a higher order sustains them and empowers them to combat M.E.E.S. The type of spiritual connection varies tremendously in our African American community. Some go to church each Sunday, some chant, some witness, some have private moments. Irrespective of one's method, it seems clear that for many, the peaceful solace of a higher order connection equips them to wage the day-to-day struggle of being black.

These strategies are not definitive. Dialogue (purposeful interaction) and research can add to these strategies. The strategies are very much intertwined. There is no one "right" way of handling M.E.E.S. What works in one situation might be tremendously wrong in another. Each person must tailor a specific "fit" in reference to his or her own needs and situation. That is not to say that there are no commonalities, there are many. We can learn about strategies through the experiences of others and our understanding of ourselves.

I suggested in the beginning of this volume that the reader would experience some of the many powerful African American lyrics through the voices and songs of a sample of my clients, family, students, peers, and friends. It is my hope that by more clearly listening to the lyrics, readers will have a better understanding of not only the negatives associated with being black in a society that has never appreciated our songs, but also the strengths and joys, the ability of some to thrive, excel, and achieve despite the odds. This brief segment of the concert is over, yet the lyrics,

    the music,

         the rhythms, and

              the beat continue.

Afterword

Race has haunted this nation since its inception. The country was born in the brutal conquest of a native people who were racially and culturally different from Europeans. Later, the United States grew strong, nurtured by the fruits from enslaved African labor and nourished by the labor of indentured Asians—both also different from Europeans. At times, however, the ever-present paradigm of racial dominance and subordination modified bizarrely to declare certain European groups "lesser races," thus making them also subject to racially inspired exploitation. The currents of racial hierarchy and its attendant racial discrimination, racial domination, and racial exploitation are deeply rooted in the history of this society.

Throughout history America has treated several categories of people as "racial victims," to a greater or lesser extent, at various points in time and over a variety of contexts. I am nevertheless compelled to argue the unique situation of African Americans. African Americans were defined as the ultimate counterpoint to Europeans—where they were free, we were slaves; they were cultured while we were labeled brutes; they were smart whereas we were considered dumb; they were beautiful and we were judged ugly. In short, under this country's racial dominance paradigm Europeans were defined as human while Africans were defined as beasts fit only to be servants to a "master race." Spoken aloud in 1997, these harsh assertions grate the ear and the conscience of right-thinking Americans. But who among us can deny the truth of these assertions about America's ugly little racial secret? To be sure such views have muted over time, softening and modifying the more extreme expressions of white supremacist thinking. In this respect much has changed for the better for blacks over the nearly four centuries since we first arrived at Jamestown, Virginia, in chains. Still, for all the changes, much remains the same.

African Americans continue to be disproportionately deprived, denied, disenfranchised, and devalued in this society. I therefore vigorously reject the new orthodoxy that claims that racial dominance/hierarchy is no longer a significant thread in the wool and weave of the American fabric. Central to this paradigm today, as it has been historically, is the notion that black people are the least among all racial and ethnic groups. In the minds of far too many Americans, blacks are seen as being at the bottom of the well and whites are seen as being at the top of the well (Bell 1992). The various other racial and ethnic groups are, in turn, seen as arrayed somewhere between the top and the bottom of the presumed natural or appropriate hierarchy. All of this leads to the undeniable conclusion that race and racism are very much real factors in the lives of most African Americans.

This books speaks eloquently and plaintively about race and racism in America. In particular the book seeks to explain how African Americans negotiate their day-to-day existence, as lived under the "shadow of whiteness." The book advances the bold assertion that to be black in America is to a priori exist in a hostile environment. Through its pages we find that the responses of African Americans to racial discrimination, denial, and devaluation are as rich and varied as the people themselves. What is constant is the reality of racial calculus in this society: race matters in ways large and small, complex and simple. Make no mistake about it, to be black in America is to bear the stigma and to feel the weight of "anti-African and Eurocentric ideas of beauty, dominance, and entitlement" (see chapter 1). American society defines black people as problems (Du Bois 1903) and life under this specter is by definition stressful.

Carroll views stress as endemic to black life in America, growing out of the treatment, perception, and images projected of African Americans in this society. In this environment racism and subtle (and often overt) oppression are ubiquitous, constant, and continuing, requiring African Americans to routinely suffer an accumulation of micro-aggressions. Examples of these racially influenced micro-aggressions against blacks include being ignored for service, being automatically associated with negatives, being treated as inferior, being treated with unwarranted suspicion, and so on.

Carroll labels the specific and cumulative effects of such micro-aggressions on African Americans as mundane extreme environmental stress (M.E.E.S.). The notion of mundane refers to the taken-for-granted, everyday nature of these pressures; extreme because of the cumulative negative impact on a person's psychological well-being, his or her worldview; environment since it arises from the context of being black in America; and stress because of the debilitating, disorienting, detracting, and degenerative effects of these factors on the person. She uses a variety of research populations—single male fathers, teen mothers, professional women, college students—to investigate mundane extreme environmental stress in the lives of African Americans across different categories and situations. What emerges are life stage, gender, class, and occupation specific narratives on racial assaults and coping strategies in the lives of African Americans. Readers are made privy to the daily confrontations of African Americans with racism (both individual and institutional) in their lives and share their triumphs and defeats in the face of this adversary. What also comes to light is a research tool for systematically incorporating the reality of mundane extreme environmental stressors into any analysis that seeks to fully understand the lives of African Americans. Not only are researchers discouraged from interpreting black life outside of the context of race and racism, but they also provided a template for assessing these effects.

This book provides a fresh new perspective on race and racism in America. For the most part scholarly literature has shied away from confronting these demons in our midst. In a few instances where the topics are considered, the tendency is to opt for analysis at the more impersonal, abstract level. The ultimate effect of such an approach is to strip away the lived, human consequences of racism. Daily insults, blocked opportunities, degradations, blows to self-confidence and self-esteem are cumulated and reduced to summary statistics. What can be lost in the process is a feeling for the person who is at the center of these interactions and who suffers the racial assaults/insults firsthand and is damaged personally by them. Where the popular literature has addressed race and racism, the results have also been lacking. These treatments have mostly been so nonrigorous, anecdotal, and impressionistic as to greatly limit their lessons for a broader understanding. The power of this book comes from its ability to weave together multiple perspectives on and approaches to the study of race, racism, and stress in the lives of African Americans.

What hope there is of resolving America's conundrum, the dilemma of race and racism, lies in first facing the problem squarely. The mundane extreme environmental stress model provides a framework and a perspective for understanding the dynamics of racism in this society. It also suggests strategies for curing this cancer in the body public. M.E.E.S. models the dynamic relationship between institutional and individual racism in America at the same time that it underscores the underlying complexities of each manifestation's sociocultural and historical roots. Stripped of pretense and rationalizations, racism is revealed as a system that does violence to the human spirit, psyche, emotions, and well-being.

Ultimately the extreme stress associated with being black in America kills, at times dramatically and publicly—as in the explosions of other-directed aggression and/or antisocial behavior gleefully reported in the news as evidence of primordial flaws in the black character. More often, however, this stress kills slowly and silently taking a long-term toll through various psychosomatic, physical ailments, as hypertension, substance abuse, low infant birth weight and high infant mortality, and poor health attitudes/behaviors that combine to give African Americans a morbidity/mortality profile more characteristic of those living in the developing world than in the industrialized world. Carroll provides firsthand testimonies by African Americans from various walks of life, testimonies that lay stark the mundane extreme environmental stress that they are forced to bear for no other reason than the fact that they happen to be African Americans. She demonstrates that the more public, high profile instances of racial discrimination—the Rodney King beating, the burning of black churches—are often but the tip of the iceberg. Beneath the surface of public consciousness, out of the media's glare, are the more numerous, insidious, persistent mundane extreme environmental stressors, the daily slights, stresses, and strains that nibble away at a person's sense of well-being.

To solve the puzzle of mundane extreme environmental stress in the lives of African Americans will ultimately benefit many others in the society. I am reminded of the tremendous ripple benefits that flowed throughout society and to specific groups—women and other minorities—as a result of changes in U.S. laws and norms brought about by the Black Civil Rights Movement. Similarly one can expect that were this country to successfully address and resolve the problem of mundane extreme environmental stress in the lives of African Americans, that is to say, were this country to change fundamentally so that blacks could live more humane, dignified existences, then the door would open for making all Americans more human. For it is a well-documented fact that "What this country would do for the least of us, i.e., African Americans, it will most certainly do for all of us" (Hare 1996). The challenge before this country now—as it was in 1776—is whether to commit wholeheartedly to the creation of a nation where the potential of all people is recognized, encouraged, and supported regardless of creed, gender, or color. Until, and unless, this goal is achieved, the United States will be judged by future generations as merely having been a glorious failure.

Walter Allen
University of California, Los Angeles

Bibliography

Akbar, N. *Chains and Images of Psychological Slavery*. Jersey City: New Mind Productions, 1984.

Allen, W. R. "The Search for Applicable Theories in Black Family Life." *Journal of Marriage and the Family* 40 (1978): 117-29.

America, R. F. *The Wealth of Races: The Present Value of Benefits from Past Injustices*. Westport, Conn.: Greenwood Press, 1990.

Aschenbrenner, J. *Lifelines: Black Families in Chicago*. New York: Holt, Rinehart & Winston, 1975.

Ashe, A., and A. Rampersad. *Days of Grace: A Memoir*. New York: Alfred A. Knopf, 1993.

Barton, K., and C. Baglio. "The Nature of Stress in Child-Abusing Families: A Factor Analytic Study." *Psychological Reports* 73 (1993): 1047-1055.

Baumrind, D. "An Exploratory Study of Socialization Effects on Black Children: Some Black-White Comparisons." *Child Development* 43 (1972): 261-67.

Bell, D. A. *Faces at the Bottom of the Well: The Permanence of Racism*. New York: Basic Books, 1992.

Billingsley, A. *Black Families in White America*. Englewood Cliffs: Prentice Hall, 1968.

___. *Climbing Jacob's Ladder*. New York: Simon and Schuster, 1992.

Blumstein, A. "Prison." In *Crime*, edited by J. Q. Wilson and J. Petersilia. San Francisco: Institute for Contemporary Studies Press, 1995.

Boykin, A. W. "Black Psychology and the Research Process: Keeping the Baby but Throwing Out the Bath Water." In *Research Direction of Black Pyschologists*, edited by A. W. Boykin, A. J. Franklin, and J. F. Yates. New York: Russell Sage Foundation, 1979.

Broderick, C. B. "Social Heterosexual Development among Urban Negroes and Whites." *Journal of Marriage and the Family* 27 (1965): 200-203.

Bruce, P. A. *The Plantation Negro as Freeman: Observation on His Character, Condition and Prospects in Virginia*. New York: G. P. Putnam's Sons, 1889.

Carew, J. V., I. Chan, and C. Halfar. *Observing Intelligence in Young Children: Eight Case Studies*. Englewood Cliffs, N.J.: Prentice-Hall, 1976.

Carew, J. V., and S. Lightfoot. *Beyond Bias: Perspectives on Classrooms*. Cambridge: Harvard University Press, 1979.

Carroll, L. *Blacks, Hacks, and Cons: Race Relations in a Maximum Security Prison*. Boston: Lexington Books, 1974.

Cary, L. *Black Ice*. New York: Knopf: Distributed by Random House, 1991.

Cazenave, N. "Black Men in America, The Quest for Manhood." In *Black Families*, edited by H. McAdoo. Beverly Hills: Sage, 1981.

Clark, K. B., and M. P. Clark. "Racial Identification and Preference of Negro Children." In *Reading in Social Psychology*, edited by E. Maccoby, T. Newcomb, and E. Hartley. New York: Holt, Rhinehart and Winston, 1958.

Coner-Edwards, A., and J. Spurlock. *Black Families in Crisis: The Middle Class*. New York: Brunner/Mazel, 1988.

Congressional Black Caucus Hearings. "Issues Forum: The Status of African American Men," September 1992.

Cooley, C. H. *Human Nature and the Social Order*. New York: Charles Scribner and Sons, 1902.

Davidson, J. National Day Care Home Study: Parent Study Component-Preliminary Report. Washington, D.C.: Department of Health, Education, and Welfare, 1978.

Debro, J. "Institutional Racism within the Justice System of American Prisons." In *Black Perspectives on Crime and the Criminal Justice System*, edited by R. L. Woodson. Boston: G. K. Hall, 1977.

Drake, S. *Black Metropolis*. London: Jonathan Cape, 1945.

Du Bois, W.E.B. *The Souls of Black Folks*. New York: Vintage Books, 1903.

Edelman, M. W. *The Measure of Our Success: A Letter to My Children and Yours*. New York: Harper Perennial, 1993.

Ellison, R. *Invisible Man*. New York: Random House, 1952.

Ewer, P., and J. O. Gibbs. "Relationship with Putative Fathers and Use of Contraception in a Population of Black Ghetto Adolescent Mothers." *Public Health Reports* 90 (1975): 417-423.

Finkel, M., and B. Finkel. "Male Adolescent Contraceptive Utilization." *Adolescence* 13 (1978): 443-451.

Garwood, A. N. *Black Americans: A Statistical Sourcebook*. Boulder: Numbers and Concepts Publishers, 1992.

Gay, G. "Cultural Difference Important in the Education of Black Children." *Momentum* October (1972): 30-33.

Genovese, E. D. *From Rebellion to Revolution: Afro-American Slave Revolts in the Making of the Modern World*. Baton Rouge: Louisiana State University Press, 1979.

Giddings, P. *When and Where I Enter: The Impact of Black Women on Race and Sex in America*. New York: Quill/W. Morrow, 1984.

Gresham, J. H. "The Politics of Family in America." *Nation* 249 (1989): 116-22.

Grief, G. L. *Single Fathers*. Boston: Lexington Books, 1985.

Grief, G. L., and A. Demaris. "Single Fathers with Custody." *Families in Society: Journal of Contemporary Human Services* 71 (1990): 259-67.

Guthrie, R. V. *Even the Rat Was White: A Historical View of Psychology.* New York: Harper and Row, 1976.

Hacker, A. *Two Nations: Black and White, Separate, Hostile and Unequal.* New York: Ballantine Books, 1992.

Hamberger, K. L., and C. Renzetti, eds. *Domestic Partner Abuse.* New York: Springer Publishing Company, 1996.

Hare, B. Personal conversation with W. Allen, 9 November 1996.

Heiss, J. *The Case of the Black Family.* New York: Columbia University Press, 1975.

Hendricks, L. E. "Suggestions for Reaching Unmarried Black Adolescent Fathers." *Child Welfare* 62 (1983): 141-46.

Hill, R. B. "Social Stress on the Family." In *Sourcebook on Marriage and the Family*, edited by M. B. Sussman. Boston: Houghton Mifflin, 1963.

___. *The Strengths of Black Families.* New York: Emerson Hill Publishers, 1972.

Hill Collins, P. *Black Feminist Thought: Knowledge, Consciousness, and the Politics of Empowerment.* Boston: Unwin Hyman, 1990.

Jackson, S., W. R. McCollough, and G. Gurin. "Family Socialization, Environment and Identity Development in Black Americans." In *Black Families*, edited by H. McAdoo. 2d ed. Newbury Park: Sage Publications, 1988.

Kanner, A. D., S. Shirley Feldman, D. A. Weinberger, and M. E. Ford. "Uplifts, Hassles, and Adaptational Outcomes in Early Adolescents." *Journal of Early Adolescents* 7, 8: 4(1987): 371-94.

Littlefield, K., and H. F. Keshet. *Fathers Without Partners.* Totowa, N.J. Rowman & Littlefield Press, 1981.

Madhubuti, H. R. *Black Men: Obsolete, Single, Dangerous-African American Men in Transition.* Chicago: Third World Press, 1990.

Malson, M. R., and B. Woody. "The Work and Family Responsibilities of Black Women Single Parents." Working paper, no. 148. Wellesley: Wellesley College, Center for Research on Women, 1985.

Malveaux, J. *Sex, Lies and Stereotypes: Perspectives of a Mad Economist.* Los Angeles: Pines Ones Publishing, 1994.

Manis, J. G., and B. N. Meltzer. *Symbolic Interaction: A Reader in Social Psychology.* Boston: Allyn and Bacon, 1967.

Marable, M. "The Black Male, Searching Beyond Stereotypes." In *The Black Family Essays & Studies*, edited by R. Staples. Belmont: Wadsworth Publishing Co., 1991.

___. "The Black Worker, an Endangered Species?: Propects for Black Labor and Economic Underdevelopment in the 1980s." Dayton: Black Research Associates, 1982.

Martin, E., and J. Martin. *The Black Extended Family.* Chicago: University of Chicago Press, 1978.

Massey, G. C. "Self-Concept Personal Control and Social Context among Students in Inner-City High Schools." Ph.D. diss., Stanford University, 1975.

Mathis, A. "Contrasting Approaches to the Study of Black Families." *Journal of Marriage and the Family* 40 (1978): 667-76.

McAdoo, H. P. "Factors Related to Upward Mobility in Black Families." *Journal of Marriage and the Family* 40 (1978): 761-68.

___. "Stress-Absorbing Systems in Black Families." Paper presented at the 1980 Groves Conference on Marriage and Family, 1980.

___. "Transgenerational Patterns of Upward Mobility in African American Families." In *Black Families*, edited by H. McAdoo. 2 ed. Newbury Park: Sage Publications, 1988.

McLloyd, V. C., and C. A. Flanagan. *Economic Stress: Effects on Family and Child Development*. San Francisco: Jossey-Bassey, 1990.

Mead, G. H. *Mind, Self and Society*. Chicago: University of Chicago Press, 1934.

Merton, R. K. *Social Theory and Social Structure*. Rev. ed. Chicago: Free Press, 1957.

Montagu, A. *Man's Most Dangerous Myth: The Fallacy of Race*. New York: Columbia University Press, 1945.

Moynihan, D. P. *The Negro Family: A Case of National Action*. Washington, D.C.: U.S. Government Printing Office, 1965.

Murphy, G. *Personality*. New York: Harper and Row, 1947.

Nelson, J. F. "Hidden Disparities in Case Processing: New York State, 1985-1986." *Journal of Criminal Justice* 20 (1992): 181-200.

Nelson, J. *Volunteer Slavery: My Authentic Negro Experience*. Chicago: Noble Press, 1993.

Nettles, M. T. "Assessing Progress in Minority Access and Achievement in American Higher Education." ECS Working Papers, PA-91-1. Denver: Education Commission of the States, 1991.

Nobles, W. "A Formulative and Empirical Study of Black Families." Report submitted to United States Department of Health, Education, and Welfare, Office of Child Development, December 1976.

Ogbu, J. U. *Minority Education and Caste: The American System in Cross-Cultural Perspective*. New York: Academic Press, 1978.

___. *The Next Generation: An Ethnography of Education in an Urban Neighborhood*. New York: Academic Press, 1974.

Pearlin, L. I. "Role Strains and Personal Stress." In *Psychosocial Stress: Trends in Theory and Research*, edited by H. B. Kaplan. New York: Academic Press, 1983.

Peters, M. F. "Nine Black Families: A Study of Household Management and Child Rearing in Black Families with Working Mothers." Ann Arbor: Xerox University Microfilms, 1976.

___. "Notes from a Guest Editor." *Journal of Marriage and the Family* 40 (1978): 655-58.

Peters, M. F., and G. C. Massey. "Mundane Extreme Environmental Stress in Family Stress Theories: The Case of Black Families in White America." In *Social Stress and the Family*, edited by H. I. McCubbin, M. B. Sussman, and J. M. Patterson. New York: the Haworth Press, 1983.

Pierce, C. M. "The Effects of Racism." Paper presented at the AMA 15th Annual Conference of State of Mental Health Representative, Chicago, 1969.

____. "The Mundane Extreme Environment and Its Effects on Learning." In *Learning Disabilities: Issues and Recommendations for Research*, edited by S. G. Brainard. Washington, D.C.: National Institute of Education, 1975.

____. "Offensive Mechanisms." In *The Black Seventies*, edited by F. Barbour. Boston: Porter Sargent, 1970.

____. "Psychiatric Problems of the Black Minority." In *American Handbook of Psychiatry*, vol. 3, edited by S. Arieti and G. Kaplan. New York: Basic Books, 1974.

Pillerman, S.L., H.F. Myers, and B.D. Smedley "Stress, Well-Being, and Academic Achievement in College." In *Black Students: Psychosocial Issues and Academic Achievement* edited by G.L. Bemy and J.K. Asamen. Newbury Park, CA: Corwim Press Inc., 1991.

Poussaint, A. "A Negro Psychiatrist Explains the Negro Psyche." In *Confrontation*, 183-84, New York: Random House, 1971.

Risman, B. J., and K. Park. "Just the Two of Us: Parent-Child Relationships in Single Parent Homes." *Journal of Marriage & the Family* 50 (1988): 1049-1063.

Russell, K., M. Wilson, and R. Hall. *The Color Complex*. New York: Harcourt Brace Jovanovich, 1992.

Salley, Columbus. *The 100 Must Read for African Americans: From the African Past to Today*. Forthcoming.

Schultz, D. "The Role of the Boyfriend in Lower-Class Negro Life." In *The Black Family: Essays and Studies*, edited by R. Staples. Belmont: Wadsworth, 1986.

Smith, A. L. "Black Adolescent Fathers: Issues for Service Provisions." *Social Work* 33 (1988): 269-71.

Spencer, M. B., G. K. Brookins, and W. R. Allen, eds. Beginnings: *The Social and Affective Development of Black Children*. Hillsdale, N.J.: Erlbaum, 1985.

Stack, C. B. *All Our Kin: Strategies for Survival in a Black Community*. New York: Harper and Row, 1974.

Stamp, K. *The Peculiar Institution: Slavery in the Antebellum South*. New York: Alfred. Knopf, 1956.

Staples, R. "Changes in Black Family Structure: The Conflict between Family Ideology and Structural Conditions." *Journal of Marriage and the Family* 47 (1985): 1005-1013.

____. *Introduction to Black Sociology*. New York: McGraw-Hill, 1976.

Steele, C. M. "Race and the Schooling of Black Americans." *Atlantic* 269 (1992): 68-77.

St. John, N. H. "The Elementary Classroom as a Frog Pond: Self-Concept, Sense of Control and Social Context." *Social Forces* 49 (1971): 581-591.

Sullivan, M. L. "Absent Fathers in the Inner City." *Annals of the American Academy of Political & Social Science* 501 (1989): 48-58.

University of California Student Profile. Office of Student Research, Berkeley: 1992.

U.S. Census, 1986.

U.S. Congress. House. Report of Select Committee on Children Youth and Families. Hearing. 101st Cong. 1st sess., 1989.

Vadies E. and D Hale.   "Attitudes of Adolescent Males toward Abortion, Contraception and Sexuality." *Social Work in Health Care* 3 (Winter 1977): 169-174.

Wacquant, L. J. D., and W. J. Wilson. "The Cost of Racial & Class Exclusion in the Inner City." *The Annals of the American Academy of Political & Social Science* 501 (1989): 8-25.

Wade-Gayles, G. J. *No Crystal Stair: Visions of Race and Sex in Black Women's Fiction.* New York: Pilgrim Press, 1984.

Wallace, M. *Black Macho and the Myth of the Superwoman.* New York: Dial Press, 1979.

Williams, P. J. *The Alchemy of Race and Rights.* Cambridge: Harvard University Press, 1991.

Wolf, M., and A. Mosnaim. *Posttraumatic Stress Disorder: Etiology, Phenomenology and Treatment.* Washington, D.C.: American Psychiatric Press, 1990.

Woodson, C. G. *The Miseducation of the Negro.* Washington, D.C.: Associated Publishers, 1933.

Index

About the Author

GRACE CARROLL is Academic Coordinator for African American Student Development, University of California, Berkeley. She has written extensively on stress and African American life.

ISBN 0-275-95929-5

4/99

15 -3/05